THE COMPLETE BOOK
OF SQUARE DANCING
(AND ROUND DANCING)

THE COMPLETE BOOK
OF SQUARE DANCING
(AND ROUND DANCING)

BETTY CASEY

University of North Texas Press
Denton, Texas

DEDICATION

With appreciation for his steadfast and steadying influence in the promotion, protection, and perpetuation of American square dancing, I gratefully
dedicate this book to Bob Osgood.

Permissions
University of North Texas Press
PO Box 311336
Denton, Texas 76203
(940) 565-2142

Library of Congress Cataloging in Publication Data

Casey, Betty.
The complete book of square dancing (and round dancing).
Bibliography: p. 185.
Includes index.
1. Square dancing. 2. Round dancing.
I. Title
GV1763.C27   793.3'4
ISBN 1-57441-119-5
Library of Congress Catalog Card Number 75-40781

Many, Many Thanks

"Everybody listens when Betty Casey calls a square dance . . ."

I appreciate the generous support of the many square and round dancers whose advice and assistance helped provide much of the material for this book, and I would like personally to thank each one. Space does not permit listing them all, but I extend extra heartfelt thanks to the following who were particularly unstinting in sharing their time and knowledge. None are in any way responsible for errors or mistakes that unknowingly I might have made in the text.

Bob Osgood, editor of *Square Dancing,* the official publication of the Sets In Order American Square Dance Society, provided back copies of the magazine for research, and authoritative overall editorial assistance and guidance. Willard Orlich, workshop editor and choreographer for *American Square Dance* magazine, was very helpful in editing the movement definitions.

Marshall Flippo volunteered the very nice Foreword and generously provided most of the material for the Patter Calls in "Selected Square Dance Calls." Melton Luttrell, C. O. Guest, and Bill Wright helped check out the teaching "calls," movements, and diagrams.

Emanuel Duming gave invaluable assistance as overall adviser and consultant for choreography. Bob Ruff made suggestions for the Introduction. Ivan Milhous spent hours proofreading, and Louis Domingues helped research old square dance calls. Dorothy Shaw allowed me to include her *Family Tree of the Dance.*

Bud and Lil Knowland, editors of *Round Dancer* magazine, contributed copyrighted material used in the section on round dancing. Norman and Helen Teague, round dance teachers, provided material from their *Manual for the Round Dancer.* Excerpts from an article published in *Canadian Dancer News* are courtesy of the author, Elisabeth Evans. Doyle and Deana Smith modeled for the Round Dance Position photographs. Manning and Nita Smith evaluated the Round Dancing section and made valuable suggestions for changes and additions.

Organizations represented by dancers and callers who patiently posed for the instructional square dance photographs carefully taken by "Fuzzy" Swayze, on the campus of Schreiner College with the kind permission of Dr. Sam M. Junkin, President, are: Hill Country Promenaders and Fritztown Squares and their caller, Harold Graham; Boerne Bunch; Alamo Stars and their caller, Emanuel Duming; and caller/president, Jay Lynn Moseley of Westerner's Square Dance Association. Students from Boerne, San Antonio, and from Notre Dame school posed for the children's photos.

The names of the square dancers are: Richard, Mary, and Dennis Herms; Dennis, Barbara, and Debby Lynn Hoerster; Archie and Doris Smith; Charlie and Ruth Weese; Clayton Kinney; Larry and Nell Taylor; Kerry Cathey; Sherri Parker; Cathy and Lori Sutton; Linda and Paul Moravits; Richard and Bonnie Duncan; Jay Lynn and Charlotte Moseley; Donna and Davi-Ann Hunter; Lynn Brasher; Ed and Norma Howell; Milton and Josephine Sherman; Dick and Alcene Rodenbeck; Phyllis Ann Burkett; Cleo Qualtrough; John Casey; Doyle and Deana Smith; John Hydrick; Tom, Cathy, and Tim Oldfield; Blayne Hopkins; John and Ruby Higens; Vivian Menefee; Allen Scarsella; Laura Davis; Dwayne Rux; Cindy Moore; Raymond Sharp; Jill Schupp; Robin Reiter; Katy Vaverek; Teresa Lopez; Rudy Garcia; Lynn Alberthal; Steven Ohlenburger; and Andrew James.

The most helpful person and the one to whom I am most indebted is my No. 1 gent, my husband, John. He has run errands, endured book research clutter in our family room and my periods of frustration, chauffeured me to interviews and special dances, laid out most of the diagrams, helped with picture-taking sessions, and posed when an extra gent was needed.

Foreword

Telling the story of square dancing requires not only much hard work but also someone who has a deep love for this great American dance.

Betty Casey has spent many years teaching and calling, not only here in the United States, but all over the globe as well. Now she has put together one of the most interesting and up-to-date books on square dancing that I have had the pleasure to read.

The following pages encompass not only the mainstream basics, with many enlightening pictures and diagrams, but also something about all aspects of square dancing—such as calling, music, round dancing, contras, sound systems, records, dress, etc.

Thanks, Betty, for such a wonderful book! Also thank you for introducing me, many years ago, to this great national dance; and also thanks from the bottom of my heart for your guidance, wonderful help, and patience when I first began to call. It became a new way of life, with uncountable pleasures and unforgettable memories.

MARSHALL FLIPPO

Contents

Introduction

The first square dance that I recall seeing was held at the annual Cowboys' Christmas Ball in Anson, Texas, in the early 1940s. It was a fascinating re-enactment in pioneer costumes (many of them authentic) of a "gay sworray" initiated at the old Morning Star Hotel in the 1800s, and immortalized in Larry Chittendon's poem by the same name:

. . . We buckled on our partners, an' tole 'em to hold on
Then shook our hoofs like lightening, until the early dawn.

Don't tell me 'bout cotillions, or germans. No sir'ree!
That whirl at Anson City just takes the cake with me.

I'm sick of lazy sufflin's, of them I've had my fill
Give me the frontier break-down, backed up by Windy Bill. . . .

Oh, Bill, I shan't forget yer, and I'll oftentimes recall,
That lively gaited sworray—"The Cowboys' Christmas Ball."

A rousing fiddle-band played traditional tunes for square dances, reels, waltzes, schottisches, polkas (danced Texas style without the hop, in deference to heavy cowboy boots), and Varsouvianna (Put-Your-Little-Foot).

From my standpoint as a previous ballroom dance instructor, the square dancing on that crowded floor was abounding bedlam. Bull-voiced callers dancing in each of twenty or thirty sets shouted different calls—all at the same time—while the band played on.

My actual participation in the activity came about a few years later in Abilene, Texas, because my daughter's Brownie Scout troop wanted to earn folk dance merit badges.

To help me out, a fellow Scout leader and her husband invited two other couples, my husband John, and me to their home for our first instructions in how to "promenade eight, 'til you get straight." We shoved aside the dining room furniture, rolled up the rug, and instead of tuning up a fiddle, we set the needle on a fast-fiddled 78 rpm recording of "Oh, Susannah." Then we "squared our set" in traditional style by one couple standing on each side of an imaginary square.

Our hostess taught, then "called" the simple geometric patterns of the figures, dancing with us at the same time. We had a great time cavorting and laughing through the dances, with more exuberance than grace. We serpentined in the "figure eight" to calls improvised and rhymed with fill-in "patter" by some long-ago cowboy.

Go around the lady, do the figure eight
Back around the gent and don't be late

Chase the rabbit, chase the squirrel
Chase the pretty girl around the world

Chase the rabbit, chase the 'coon
Chase that big boy around the room.

As our forefathers had done, we followed the call "forward six and fall back six," then we "promenaded home." I figured that was enough material to take care of my troop's needs, so that was the end of that.

I was wrong. It was only the beginning. An exciting recreational development was poised to sweep like a cool breeze on a hot day into my life and the lives of many people of the nation and the world.

The Scouts liked square dancing so much that in the interest of research for more material, John and I visited a small group meeting in someone's garage. Although practicing in casual clothing, some were members of the Abilene Square Dance Set, who did precision exhibition dances in costume under the direction of Bob Sumrall.

Bob was a veteran caller who had learned calling and dancing from old-time cowboys on open Texas ranges when he was a youngster. He intoned the "calls" in driving auctioneer cadence to recorded traditional tunes. We "caged the bird," looked around a couple to "take a peek," and repeated the "do si do" Texas style (now called do paso) until Bob ran out of rhymes.

Do si do and a little more dough
Chicken in the bread pan peckin' out dough

Granny will your dog bite, "No chile no"
One more change and on you go.

In unison the dancers did a special, swift, smooth two-step (later known as the "Abilene lift"). Eight pairs of hands met at the same time in the grapevine-like weaving of the "right and left grand," and their "two-hand" swings were graceful turnings with pinwheel-like balance. (This delicate balance was necessary when wearing costumes, so that ankle-length satin dresses would float evenly over hooped petticoats without dragging on the floor.) Joyful shouts and cowboy yells expressed the pleasure of the dancers, and an occasional solo jig provided star status for the especially talented or energetic.

Before the evening ended, we got the feel of the dance. The rhythm, the geometric symmetry, the synchronization of spirited music and movements all came together in a sense of compelling satisfaction. We were hooked.

We learned everything we could about the activity and recruited everyone we could to join us in the pleasures of this delightful discovery—and we're still at it some thirty years later.

As those before us who had passed this folk art down by word of mouth, and as others were doing in little out-of-the-way pockets of America, we shared our fun and meager knowledge with friends we cajoled into letting us show them how to schottische and "make a right-hand star howdy do, then back with the left and how are you?" I did the calling.

We formed the Circle Eight Club of two sets, or squares. Members sought new material from old-timers and the few books available,

and took turns teaching and "shouting" the calls so both squares could hear, often dancing in one of them at the same time.

John, who is a radio engineer, built me a public-address system combining a record player, loudspeakers, and a microphone. Wider-voice coverage via the mike enabled us to enlarge our club membership, and me to set up classes for adults and children (including our three—Rosanne, Ben, and Tom).

Our chief problem was getting suitable music. Recorded traditional square dance tunes were played at a fast speed geared more to displaying the talent of the musicians than to dancing. Early recordings that included the voiced "call" had the same drawback; time was not allowed for completion of the movements. On special open dance nights the club hired a fiddle band, rented a hall, and invited dancers from surrounding communities. Everyone who knew a call took part in the program.

Square dance costumes were another challenge. It was met variously by individual taste and sewing ability.

For women, copies of hot, hobbling pioneer homespuns and ankle-length pantaloons, or cumbersome floor-length satin skirts over hooped petticoats soon gave way to more functional full-circle midcalf-length ballerina skirts. These too had a drawback. A vigorous twirl sent the skirts flying in revealing flares. One embarrassed woman, realizing she was exposed to the waist, made things worse—she squatted down. The skirt folded over her head. Pantaloons were reinstated in shortened form.

Later, today's comfortable, colorful costume evolved. Full-skirted, tiered, or gored dresses with lace and ruffled trim float gracefully over bouffant matching nylon petticoats (some have sixty yards of material), revealing an occasional glimpse of modest matching fitted lace-trimmed thigh-length "pettipants."

Men's costumes went from plaid sport shirts and Levi's to satin shirts with dress trousers and bright neckerchiefs, to today's handsome tailored stockman pants and fitted, long-sleeved western shirts worn with bolo, string, or gambler ties.

Women wore street shoes or ballet slippers; and many men, unaccustomed to cowboy boots, proudly limped onto the floor shod in elaborately stitched high-heeled and pointed-toed beauties with their pants legs stuffed into the tops cowboy style.

Later, square dance slippers for women in many colors, with straps over the insteps, and a shortened dance boot for men were specially manufactured. Some men still prefer cowboy boots.

I was soon able to call more than two hundred figures (entire dances), and students clamored for written instructions. In 1949 I published a little red handbook called *Square Dance Instructions*. Similar developments were occurring all over America.

As hundreds of couples in my classes responded to the joyous satisfactions of square dancing, my own pleasure in it and dedication to it increased. Introduction to this versatile, enjoyable recreation had a good influence and far-reaching effects on many of my students' lives.

A young husband who had been a reluctant participant in the lessons said, "You can chalk a big one up to square dancing—it saved our marriage." Previously he had spent his spare time on stag fishing and hunting trips, and his lonely wife had been on the verge of leaving him, before they found a recreational activity to enjoy together.

A wife whose husband had a weakness for alcohol said, "I'm delighted to say that he's hardly uncapped a bottle since we started square dancing." A kindly gray-haired grandfather with a twinkle in his eye said, "Miss Betty, I thank you. This is the most fun my wife and I have had since our courting days." A busy doctor told me, "It's the only thing I do that blots out the cares of my practice for a while."

The mother of a third-grader said, "Dickey's grades are better because square dancing has given him increased confidence and self-esteem."

Some students learned a call or two and called on dance programs at open dances held in my Square Dance Center for previous students and their friends. One of these, Marshall Flippo, went on to become the top national traveling caller.

Have I had problems as a result of being a woman in a position usually held by men? Usually not, but I have to chuckle about one incident involving a bit of male chauvinism.

One of my students, a would-be caller, published a book of pictures of callers, their favorite calls, and a listing of open dances across the land. My name was not in the book (nor was any other woman's). Since my policy was to support all square dance promotions, I announced to my dancers that the book was available.

But I wasn't magnanimous enough to let him get off scot free. When his turn at the mike came, without his knowing it, I adjusted the sound to make his voice sound terrible. As far as I know, he never found out.

Most men square dance leaders have accepted me on the basis of whatever talent or accomplishment I showed, and some have been downright chivalrous. The late Dr. Lloyd "Pappy" Shaw was one of these.

I first heard of his Colorado Springs Cheyenne Mountain School summer classes in 1949 from a visitor to one of my dances. "Betty," she said, "since you are so interested in square dancing, why don't you go to Dr. Shaw's classes and really learn about it?"

Learn about it? I almost had apoplexy. I taught large classes night after night and had sold my square dance book in thirty-four states. After I simmered down, I applied for admission to a class that was to begin within a few weeks. Pappy had heard of my book, so his reply read, ". . . have just had a cancellation, happy to have you fill it—but please don't tell any of those on the waiting list."

At Pappy's I learned that my proud knowledge was limited to one of many regional types of dancing; and I was inspired by his magnificent philosophy toward life in general and preservation of American heritage through square dancing. I also earned an accolade—for being the caller who made the most improvement! I returned to my classes with new and wider square dance horizons for the movement, which expanded and modernized from that time on.

In 1953 my husband's work assignment took our family overseas for several years—to Asia, Europe, and Africa. Wherever we went, interest in learning to square dance was universally high among Americans overseas and natives of the countries we visited. It was an exciting way of sharing American culture with foreign friends, sometimes under unusual circumstances.

In the Philippines during a tourist visit to Iwahig Penal Colony deep in the jungles on Palawan island, Major Andres, the dignified director, said, "I've always wanted to see square dancing. Would it be possible for you to show us?"

"Certainly," I replied. "Could we have some music? Perhaps a guitar?"

"Would a band do?" he asked.

The "Texas Star" has seldom been danced in stranger circumstances. Since it was court day at the colony, there were judges and visiting dignitaries who "squared up" as partners for the Filipino and American women in our group, while a full band, complete with orange prison suits, played the accompaniment.

I called for Americans to dance on the Fourth of July program at the U. S. Embassy in Manila and at the Brussels World's Fair. I taught Filipino girls and German *frauleins* who danced with American G.I.s and sailors at USOs, Service Clubs, and on American carriers. I presented American teen-age dancers on television in Manila, Hong Kong, and Munich, and in a Western movie in Germany; and held classes at *Amerika Haus* in Munich for German and American youth groups.

The language barrier brought about some amusing situations. Once at a YMCA dance in Hong Kong, I called in English, and an interpreter repeated the calls in Chinese; and in Saigon, an earnest Vietnamese woman with limited command of English introduced me as "a famous call lady."

After returning to the United States in the sixties a leg injury kept me out of dancing for a few years. When able to dance again, I looked with fresh appreciation at exciting, challenging, and sophisticated changes in my favorite recreation. It had become a full-grown national pastime enjoyed by an estimated six million dancers.

As consultant to Dr. Ralph Steele, co-ordinator of curriculum in parks, recreation, and conservation (later also with the Institute of Coastal and Marine Reserves) at East Carolina University, I was dismayed to learn of his difficulty in getting updated reference material to use in square dance classes—classes that were designed to introduce students to the activity and help them "catch the spirit of square dancing."

"A complete, updated book on modern square dancing is needed," Dr. Steele said.

I discovered that there was not a single book that explained everything about modern square and round dancing. There were excellent periodicals and small handbooks available from specialized sources. Most were for people already familiar with modern square dancing, and were divided into pamphlets on individual aspects of the activity.

I decided that this book needed to be written. It is a concise, streamlined reference book with step-by-step instructions for modern square and round dance fun for everyone.

It is for people in search of material for square dance parties, club western nights, or Boy or Girl Scout merit badges; for teachers needing instructions on how to prepare and present square dance demonstrations on programs; and for recreation directors setting up square dance classes. It is also for folks wanting to learn to square dance or to call; and for square dancers who would like to organize a class or club, or review a specific movement.

This book contains "everything you need to know" to have a great time square dancing with your friends. Square dancing is friendship set to music. Happy square dancing!

Betty Casey

THE COMPLETE BOOK
OF SQUARE DANCING
(AND ROUND DANCING)

I

BACKGROUND OF THE MODERN
AMERICAN SQUARE DANCE

Genealogical Chart (1450 — Present)

The Ancestry of American Square Dancing

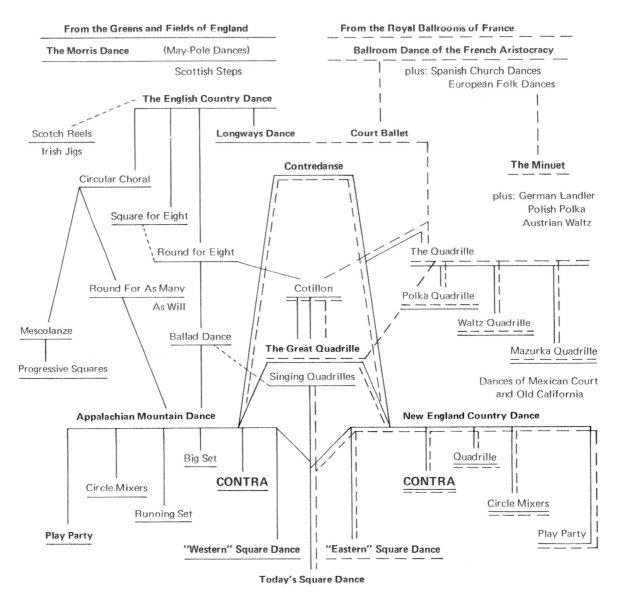

From **The Story of Square Dancing**—*A Family Tree by Dorothy Shaw, published by The Sets in Order American Square Dance Society, Los Angeles, California.*

Today's Square Dances Are Different

The square dance is a lively traditional American folk dance enjoyed by Americans, young and old, since pioneer days.

But Modern Square Dancing is Different.

The difference compares with that between clopping along by horse and buggy on a lonely country road, and negotiating rush-hour freeway traffic in a high-powered car. Most of the change has occurred since the end of World War II.

Square dancing, old style or modern, is performed to a wide variety of rhythmic tunes, by "sets" or "squares" made up of four couples whose movements are directed by a "caller." The caller chants, says, or sings the square dance calls. The movement patterns range from simple to complicated geometric designs —lines, stars, circles, squares, and cloverleaves. Dancers familiar with the language of square dancing, the dancer designations, and the movements, can perform a wide variety of patterns. This is the essence of square dancing.

Early settlers jolted across hill and dale by wagon and buggy to attend barn raisings, quilting bees, and weddings in isolated areas scattered throughout the sparsely settled West. Afterward, crowded into a kitchen or a barn, in happy sociability, someone might fiddle a thin but rollicking "Turkey in the Straw" or "Old Joe Clark" hoedown. With rough grace, hardy frontiersmen in buckskins set the girls' curls and long narrow calico skirts to bouncing in highly regionalized versions of America's frontier dance, in response to a volunteer caller's impromptu shout.

Swing your little sage-hen 'round and 'round
'Til the heel of your boot makes a hole in the
    ground.

Today, spacious floors overflow with kaleidoscopic color created by masses of smooth-stepping, smartly dressed, trained dancers assembled from far and near by auto, train, or plane, all performing together a standardized, modernized version of square dancing. On these festive occasions dancers wear special clothing that has come to be recognized as the costume for square dancing. Men wear tailored western shirts, ties, and trousers; ladies deck themselves in pretty, functional, full-skirted, knee-length dresses over fluffy rainbow-hued petticoats made of synthetic miracle fabrics.

The old-time fiddler and live musicians have been largely replaced by special full-band square dance recordings of current and traditional tunes. Large halls resound to the voices of professional articulate trained callers, accompanied by a variety of recorded tunes— current, popular, or western hits, Broadway tunes, and well-played old-time favorites. Some tunes that have been popular are "Hello, Dolly!," "Mack the Knife," and "Gentle on My Mind." These are amplified by powerful portable electronic public-address systems designed to meet the special needs of square dancing.

The American square dance is different from other folk dances. It is the only one always directed by a caller who exercises the prerogative of extemporaneously choosing patterns from known basic movements and terminology, or making up new ones of original combinations for the dancers to follow. Since square dance movements have no set patterns, within the four-couple-caller format, new movements and calls are constantly evolving.

There is leeway for great variation in the choice of music, makeup of figures, actual footwork and hand positions used, and in colorful social and regional expressions woven into the calls.

Rope the cow, brand the calf
Swing your honey once and a half.

The constantly changing façade of the square dance keeps it ever contemporary and enjoyable. Formal calls to "honor your lady," a holdover from courtly quadrilles, have joined smoothly with "barbed wire fence and a great big gate, promenade eight 'til you get straight," improvised by lusty cowboys, and "slip the clutch" or "spin chain the gears," contributed by freeway fans.

The square dance is uniquely American. Vibrant strands of Americana woven into the dance represent historical development and background of the American way of life—from homespun to wash-and-wear. The format, many of the folk dance movements, and the terminology incorporated into the square dance were brought by early emigrants from other countries to the United States. Borrowed bits from foreign dances such as French quadrilles, Irish jigs, English reels, and Spanish fandangos have blended with American folkways and customs into the square dance.

Settlers in the New England area perpetuated precise measured European court quadrilles danced in a square formation, and contras, or country dances, done from facing lines and following set patterns called out by a prompter. The Appalachian mountain region contributed the running set, an exuberant English folk dance formed by one large circle of couples who follow figures freely chosen by a caller. Dancers in western states—Texas, Colorado, California, and others—fused the square formation of the quadrille and figures from contras with the lively freedom of movement in the running set. This hybrid was called the western square dance for a time and later became known simply as the modern American square dance.

Resourceful pioneers in isolated settlements combined the remembered fragments of folk dances from their native lands with their own original additions into regional square dance figures that varied widely. These variations were only occasionally introduced into new regions by itinerants or new settlers, and even then, seldom in original form.

Prompters or callers chanted or sang gay improvised directions for the made-up figures and filled in with partly-rhymed colorful "patter" to allow time for execution of the dance, to count out the beat, and to cover up errors. Rhythmic accompaniment was composed of

hand clapping or tunes from the old countries or toe-tapping hoedowns—with probable Negro origins—played on fiddle, fife, piano, banjo, dulcimer, guitar, or harmonica.

Movements for early-day dances were easy and simple enough to master during an evening's dancing. Some calls were clearly directional, as: "Bow to your lady and give her a swing." Some incorporated terms depicting local life or settings; for example: ". . . Swing your little sage-hen," or "Swing the girl from Arkansas," or "Swing Grandma."

Others used special terminology from foreign folk dances and sometimes corruptions of foreign expressions. The word *allemande* in the call "allemande left" is thought to be a holdover from a very old German folk dance by the same name. The call directs a man and the lady at his left to swing with the left hand or arm. "Do sa do" (not to be confused with do si do), is a corruption of the French term *dos à dos,* meaning back to back, as it directs facing dancers to move forward and pass all the way around each other back to back.

There were some calls with hidden meanings. In the following one, "cornbread" denotes a two-hand swing described as "decent," while "biscuit" is a more intimate waist-swing.

Meet your honey, pat her on the head
If she don't like biscuit, give her cornbread.

These expressions developed a special square dance language. Figures, specific dance patterns, for the regional dances, became set for each entire square dance call, and went by names such as "The Arkansas Traveler," "The Texas Star," "Cage the Bird," or "The Cowboy Loop."

First old couple, bow and swing
Lead to the couple at the right of the ring

Circle four in the middle you do
Couple three arch and four trail through

Turn right around, and go back through
Tie that knot like the cowboys do.

Early figures repeated the simple movements for each of the four couples in turn to execute with all other couples in the square. Usually between the turns for individual couples, there was a fill-in movement that involved all the dancers, such as "grand right and left." An introductory call, as "Bow to your partners and swing/Then all circle left around the ring," and an ending, completed the dance. The caller was free to choose the fill-in, introductory, and ending "calls" to go with the set figures.

Ladies to their seats and gents all foller
Thank the fiddler and kiss the caller.

Some early square dance calls were sung. Specific patterns, or figures, were named after particular old-time tunes. Examples are "Red River Valley," "Red Wing," and "Darling Nellie Gray." Most square dances, however, were done to patter calls chanted in time to any "hoedown" tune with duple rhythm. Some of the tunes were "Buffalo Gal," "Soldier's Joy," "Hen and Chickens," and "Boil Them Cabbages Down." Some, known as waltz quadrilles, were set to waltz time.

Dance steps were widely varied for the regional types of square dancing in vogue before post World War II. The steps ranged from jigging, skipping, energetic Appalachian mountain clogging, which is featured on today's Grand Ole Opry television shows, to fast Texas two-stepping possibly influenced by the polka or the spirited Spanish fandango step, and the effortless gliding walk danced in California and Colorado. Appropriately timed solo jigs and individual interpretations by dancers were encouraged.

Couple dances like the two-step, schottische, polka, and waltz were alternated with square dances on an evening's program. The Virginia reel and other line dances were also popular in many areas.

The stylized elegance and measured steps of early European dances had a brief time in the sun among the elite during the twenties. Old-fashioned contras, quadrilles, and minuets were revived, and recorded in a well-researched book, *Good Morning,* published in 1926 by Mr. and Mrs. Henry Ford.

A few years before World War II, there was a significant development in Colorado. The late Dr. Lloyd "Pappy" Shaw, then a school superintendent, introduced European and American folk dancing to his students. He had searched the nooks and crannies of the nation, from the East Coast to the West Coast, collect-ing authentic folk dances, music, and square dance figures.

He published these findings, along with his eloquent philosophy emphasizing the significance of square and round dancing in American heritage, in two excellent books: *Cowboy Dances* (1939) and *The Round Dance Book* (1948).

In *Cowboy Dances* he said, "The time seems ripe for a revival. . . . They [the old square dances] are a living bit of the colorful days of the Old West. Beaten out by hand in the crude forge room of necessity, they are an authentic witness of the life of our fathers . . . fashioned from old fragments of dances that had been carried by ox team from many lands. Perhaps one day they will all quiet down to one great American folk-dance form."

Pappy discovered the differences in movements and terms used in regional dances, and the limited knowledge of many callers conducting square dances at that time in bars, barns, grange halls, and family kitchens. Also he observed that in the past, rowdiness and drinking, synonymous with square dancing in some places, had caused the quality of dancing to degenerate.

He felt it important to rescue the once extensive and highly acceptable activity not only for the enjoyment of his students, but also for America. Dr. Shaw shared his findings in classes for his school students and also offered summer classes for dancers, callers, and national leaders in the fields of folk dancing, teaching, and recreation. The summer students returned to hometowns, cities, and hamlets to share their knowledge and Pappy's philosophy with eager dancers through organized classes.

After World War II it seemed that everyone wanted to learn to square dance, and the movement rose to a crescendo of fad proportions. No one knows exactly why. Perhaps it was because as hostilities phased out, war-weary, fun-hungry people were eager to make new friends and develop new recreational skills, to relax and laugh again. Returning servicemen united with wives and sweethearts in their hometowns—deep in mountain hollows, high on windswept plains, and in the lowlands along sandy seashores—discovered the refreshing charisma of early regional square dancing.

Existing square dance groups expanded, others were organized, and square dancing moved to larger and more generally acceptable meeting places such as community, school, and church recreation halls. Better public-address systems, with their record players and microphones, and special square dance recordings made it possible for callers to handle the larger crowds.

Soon simple repetitive figures no longer satisfied dancers who had memorized them all. The search for new material was on in earnest, but very little was available. Callers exchanged material, improvised, and devised more challenging dances utilizing intermingling figures and introducing new coined terminology and movements—such as "allemande thar," "cross trail," and "wheel and deal." Singing calls were choreographed to fit tunes such as "My Little Girl" and "Oh, Johnny, Oh." The audacious dared to turn to catchy ragtime rhythm. The first was written to the tune of "Alabama Jubilee" by Joe Lewis, a Texas caller.

Cars, good roads, and shorter working hours provided convenient transportation and more leisure time for dancing. As dancers from different areas got together they too discovered the problems caused by differences in regional styles and performance.

For instance, in one area, in response to the call "Go all around your left-hand lady," the gent passed in front of the lady. Fifty miles away, the gent went behind her. Result? Collision. No one had the authority to decide which interpretation was the "right" way, so for a while many areas held stubbornly to their own regionalisms (some still do), and tempers flared hotly in the give and take of reaching compromises. One old-time caller who was convinced that his interpretation was "the" way was heard to declare flatly, "If you're not a-doin' it the way I'm tellin' you, you're not square dancin'."

Another example involved the difference in movements danced to the call "do si do." In Colorado the particular movements danced to the call "do si do" limited its performance to two couples. Texas square dancers performed a simple but versatile "do si do" pattern involving two or more couples. Georgians called the Texas "do si do" figure "Georgia rangtang."

After Dr. Shaw had seen the Texas figure

danced at Herb Greggerson's square dance barn in El Paso, in order for his dancers to use it without confusion, he called it "do paso" after that city. Eventually, after many hot arguments, the Colorado figure retained the name of "do si do." This arbitrarily standardized and clarified the two calls and movements, yet it practically eliminated the well-known Texas-style "do si do" calls, since the Colorado movement is seldom danced.

Do si do don't you know
You can't catch a rabbit 'till it comes a snow

Do si do on a heel and toe
It's one more change then home you go.

Square dancing contests were popular in some parts of the country in the years following World War II. This practice had some good and some bad results. It promoted smoother, more rhythmic dancing; careful attention to costumes; and discriminating selection of movements that flowed in pleasing patterns. On the other hand, it presented square dancing as a spectator activity; caused hard feelings among the losers, discouraged participation by those with less dexterity; and promoted competitive attitudes.

Many square dance leaders objected to the idea of competition, holding that the folk activity should be kept open for participation enjoyment by all. They encouraged demonstrations and exhibitions instead. Leaders also resisted commercialization by sponsorship or advertisements, especially if the promotion connected square dance activities with alcoholic beverages.

During the quarter century following World War II, drastic changes occurred and American square and round dancing took on a new look. In the early fifties, the trend moved away from the set patterns of figures in patter calls into free-style "hash" combinations of individual movements in the figures. Before, an entire patter call went under a single name (Texas Star, Arkansas Traveler) and had a set choreography except for the fill-in, introduction, and ending. For "hash" calling each movement in the figure stood alone, to be combined with selected movements from other figures. This opened the door to innumerable combinations that gave callers free reign over extemporaneous composition of a square dance call and challenged dancers to pay strict attention. It was no longer possible for them to memorize the choreography. Les Gotcher, a Texas and California caller, was among the first callers to promote "hash" calling nationally.

Many new singing calls were choreographed to popular tunes. Few survived in original form, as they soon became outdated by changes in calling terminology.

Instruction books and pamphlets with the new calls and directions were printed and distributed, and square dance periodicals were begun. These facilitated the rapid exchange of material.

Among the most authoritative and influential instructions for callers were those by the late Ed Gilmore, a California caller. He outlined standard criteria for timing calls and synchronizing them with movements and music.

The speed of square dancing accelerated. The dance step settled into a swift, smooth, gliding walk without skips or jerks, which adapts best to the faster tempo.

Members of dance classes organized into clubs with regular meeting nights. The club became the basic structure of the square dance world, functioning as the chief sponsoring agent for classes ever bringing new dancers into the activity. Minimal dues were set to defray the cost of the hall and the caller. Square dance organizations blossomed everywhere—for couples, singles, youth, children, and campers. Square dance classes, clubs, and associations were organized on local, state, national, and international levels.

The people who flocked to square dance classes did not know how to do the old-time couple dances, called round dances in Pappy's book, so callers and teachers learned them, then "cued" the dancers through them. To make teaching easier, specific dance choreography was set to specific tunes, as "The Beer Barrel Polka" or "The Third Man Theme." The caller "cued" the steps for all couples, who followed each other around in a circle doing the same steps simultaneously. Thus a new dance form—"cued" round dancing (now referred to simply as round dancing)—was born. Round dancing is an integral part of the square dance activity.

Some of these "rounds," such as "Patty Cake Polka" and "Waltz of the Bells," were choreographed to include constantly changing partners. These are known as mixer rounds.

New round dances were choreographed to available recorded tunes by callers and dancers almost as fast as were new square dances. Most callers were unable to keep abreast of the flood of new material, so special teachers for round dancing developed. A few of these had ballroom and foreign folk dance backgrounds, but they were mostly from the ranks of round dancing square dancers.

Among the outstanding early leaders in the field were Frank and Carolyn Hamilton. Frank has written several instruction books on the subject. The latest is *Roundance Manual* for the Sets in Order American Square Dance Society.

From these self-made teachers came a rash of rounds choreographed to every conceivable rhythm—rhumba, foxtrot, waltz, cha cha, tango, and swing. They borrowed ballroom and foreign folk dance terminology and abbreviations, and made up others for use in teaching.

Many of the dances were too complicated to learn in the limited time allotted them at square dances. Eventually, separate clubs were organized for round dancing only. Then, to keep round dancing in the square dance picture, leaders established a system of classifying easier dances as square dance rounds, leaving the more difficult ones for round dance clubs. Two outstanding leaders, Manning and Nita Smith, have helped set the pace in the development of round dancing since the forties, especially in the area of square dance rounds. Widely known for fine choreography in the dances they have written, they are sought out to conduct workshops across the nation and around the world. In 1963, the editors of *Round Dancer Magazine,* Bud and Lil Knowland, began polling their readers to determine the most popular and enduring dances. These are now limited to fifteen dances and are known as "classic rounds."

Today callers often learn and teach the square dance rounds to their clubs and classes. Sometimes a club has a separate round dance teacher.

To meet the specialized needs of square and

round dance programs for a constant, appropriate supply of recorded music, square dance recording companies were established. They provide music for round dancing, some with the music with voiced cues on one side and without the cues on the flip side; and square dance records with music accompanied by the voiced "calls" on one side and without the voice on the other. Callers and teachers can learn from the side with the cues or "calls," then play the flip side, accompanied by their own voices for the dancers to follow.

Now there are weekend square and round dance teaching institutes for callers and dancers. Vacation spots across the nation feature organized square and round dance workshops for dancers. Through caller training workshops, known as callers schools or colleges, many callers have attained part- or full-time professional status. Others have become full-time traveling callers, booking engagements for large special dances and festivals across America and even overseas. Outstanding callers have established note services for other callers.

Annual national square dance conventions were begun in 1952 and have been held each year in different cities—from Anaheim to Atlantic City and from Salt Lake City to San Antonio. Attendance has ranged from twelve thousand to twenty-two thousand enthusiastic dancers joyfully following amplified chants into challenging and complex geometric patterns. The twenty-fifth National Square Dance Convention, scheduled to be held in June 1976 in Anaheim, California, is designated an official Bicentennial celebration.

Many festivals, association dances, and the dances at the national conventions follow a round-robin type of programming, with volunteer callers contributing their skills for the enjoyment of all.

Side two couples square through. . . .
Then you do the curlique

Swing through, centers run like that
Then wheel and deal and box the gnat.

By the late fifties, an expanded but fairly stable basic language had evolved and generally was adopted by square dancers across the land—and the sea. Americans took square dancing with them to the far corners of the earth and shared it with people everywhere. Square dance clubs were organized from Europe to Asia. It is estimated that there are 12,000 clubs in the United States, 700 in Canada, 100 in England, 82 in Japan, and 100 in Australia. There are many others in the 50 countries where square dancing is enjoyed.

In 1958, 101 American dancers and six callers—5 men and a woman (the author.—Editor)—presented square dancing in front of the United States pavilion at the Brussels World's Fair. Thus the movement had symbolically come full cycle. The fragmented foreign folk dances that had found their way to the frontiers of early America had winged their way back home like boomerangs—in new and exciting forms.

Then new problems developed. A wide gap appeared between the dancing skill and repertoire of those who had years of dancing experience and leisure to dance several nights weekly, and others just getting started, or unable to dance often. Also, a flood of new expressions and movements being introduced by the large numbers of callers caused confusion and dismay. Versatility, the appealing factor that allowed for development of new terminology and movements, became a threatening monster. The basic vocabulary used in pioneer square dancing had expanded into a specialized organized program claiming more than a thousand movements. (Sach's *World History of the Dance* reports that Playford's *English Dancing Master* [eighteenth edition, 1728] describes nine hundred country dances, but no one was expected to know more than a few of them.)

As a means of paving the way for a program of "square dancing to meet the needs of everyone," Bob Osgood, editor of a national square dance magazine, *Sets in Order,* now called *Square Dancing,* spearheaded a study that resulted in the introduction of a new concept of organized square dance presentation in 1969.

Square dance experts made up a committee that studied many facets of square dancing, and organized the Sets in Order American Square Dance Society (SIOASDS). SIOASDS is dedicated to the promotion, protection, and perpetuation of American square dancing.

This committee designed a two-pronged

plan. One was to establish and promote standardization of teaching procedures, terminology, and movements. The other divided square dance basic movements into segments intended to promote three plateaus (skill levels) of square dancing in order to meet different needs of the dancers.

From long-established square dance practices, SIOASDS chose fifty and published a booklet called *The Basic Movements of Square Dancing—Basic 50,* suitable for those dancing on the first-plateau level.

Later, twenty-five other movements were selected and printed in another booklet called *The Extended Basic Movements of Square Dancing (51–75),* to be added to the first fifty for use in the second plateau.

The third plateau was labeled experimental and challenge dancing. It incorporates ever-new and challenging combinations of movements under coined names.

In 1974 there were other developments. Ten more movements were added to the list by SIOASDS, to be incorporated somewhere between the second and third skill levels. Another national magazine, *American Square Dance,* edited by Stan and Cathie Burdick, published the last ten movements in a listing from a booklet called *Plus-50 Experimental Movements,* written by the magazine's workshop editor, Willard Orlich.

And the Association of Square Dance Callers, under the name CALLERLAB, had its first annual convention. It was attended by some one hundred invited square dance callers and leaders. Fourteen committees discussed subjects such as communication, cultural exchange, caller benefits and accreditation, contracts, ethics, ways to control the unrestricted flow of new movements, and standardization.

This approach helped to establish general guidelines standardizing the fundamental language and basics of square dancing without destroying the caller's freedom to choose the movements he or she integrates into "calls." No distinct lines are drawn for the plateaus, or levels, of dancing—only general ones dependent on the inclination and ability of the caller-teacher and the dancers. About eighty-five selected movements now make up the *Mainstream Movements* of modern square dancing.

As the result of standardization, enjoyable differences in dancing, such as two-stepping, extra hand-clapping, and preferred language for favorite calls, are discouraged, although still indulged in by a few individualists. But standardization makes it possible for one to square dance comfortably anywhere in the world.

Regional types of square dances are still around, and folks get together for party square dancing based on old-time and simple figures —at vacation camps, Scout meetings, and socials. But the organized version of modern American square dancing is the big one—the one that draws the crowds of dancers.

Although enjoyable to watch, square dancing is not a spectator sport. It is a vital and challenging participation activity. You too can join the fun—learn to square dance or to call —by following the step-by-step instructions for the eighty-five *Mainstream Movements,* in this book.

Now it's time to

Wipe off your tie, pull down your vest
And dance with the one you love the best.

II

MODERN SQUARE DANCING

. . . STEP BY STEP

85 Mainstream Movements with Calls

It has been said that "Anyone who can walk can enjoy modern square dancing." Lessons are necessary, but it is easy to learn. It is a comparatively inexpensive, enjoyable recreation—from the first hesitant "do sa do" through completing a course of lessons, joining a club, and confidently entering the pleasurable world of friendly square dancers everywhere.

There are only four requirements for having a good time square dancing. They are: four male-female couples for each "set" or "square"; smooth floor space; lively music, and an enthusiastic and knowledgeable caller/teacher.

The dancers may be any age, size, or shape. Floor space might be in a dining room with furniture pushed aside, at a church or school recreation hall, or on a patio—so long as it is large enough for all participating sets simultaneously to join extended hands in individual circles.

Music, recorded or played live in duple time, should have a strong, steady rhythm at about 128 to 132 metronome beats per minute. Special square dance records are recommended.

Most important is the caller/teacher. He or she must have command of the special terminology of the language of square dancing and know the movements with their appropriate "calls" for dancers to follow. The caller from a local square dance club may be hired to teach, or the leader of the group may teach and call.

Here are eighty-five *Mainstream Movements* of modern square dancing, with instructions for learning to dance them. Diagrams and photographs make the explanations easy to understand, and there is a sample "teaching call" with each movement demonstrating *one of many ways* it may be used. (Asterisked substitutions demonstrate some other ways the movement may be used.) Each of the "calls" begins and ends with dancers in home positions. In the calls, active dancer designations and the movement being introduced are italicized.

The presentation begins with easy basic movements and progresses to high-skill-level patterns. The movements are arranged in a simple step-by-step consecutive pyramid learning order, and are also listed and numbered separately for easy use and reference.

Following the explanations of the movements, there is a collection of calls for modern square dancing in which various movements are choreographed into complete square dances. These arrangements typify square dancing as it is done today.

There is also a section called "The Special Language of Square Dancing: A Selected Glossary," which explains special square dance terms.

So:

Promenade that girl in blue
Then the one with a rundown shoe.

"One more couple over here . . ."

1 SQUARE YOUR SETS

A preliminary "call" chanted in rhythm to the music to summon dancers into four-couple "sets" or "squares" on the floor. If a square is incomplete, those already in place should hold up fingers indicating the number of dancers or couples needed to complete it. (Squares may also be formed by other means, such as dancing the "Grand March" or taking four-couple segments from a large circle.)

CALL

All square your sets around the hall
Four couples to a set, listen to the call.

Square your sets

Note

Each couple (with the lady at the gent's right side) stands in place in the middle of one side of an imaginary square that lines up with sides of the dance area. To establish proper spacing, dancers extend their arms just above an average waist height and join hands in a comfortable circle; then drop hands and step nearer to partners. Joining hands will not be necessary after dancers learn to take proper places automatically. The square thus formed will be about ten to twelve feet across. Movements should be danced within this approximate space.

Square formation

All dancers have name and number designations in the square formation and in relation to each other. Every dancer must be thoroughly familiar with these designations. For *Home Position* designations, the couples are numbered counterclockwise from one (1) to four (4). *Couple 1* stands with their backs toward the caller and/or music. *Couple 2* stands to the right of *Couple 1*. *Couple 3* faces *Couple 1*; and *Couple 4* faces *Couple 2*.

Opposites are couples or individuals facing each other at a given time. From *Home Positions* the following are *Opposites*. Couples 1 and 3 are *Opposites* for each other and are also called *Head Couples*. Individual *Opposites* are: Lady 1 and Gent 3; Gent 1 and Lady 3. *Couples 2* and *4* are *Opposites* for each other, and are also called *Side Couples*. Individual *Opposites* are: Lady 2 and Gent 4, Gent 2 and Lady 4.

The person to the gent's left, or to the lady's right in a square or circle formation, is called their *Corner*.

From *Home Positions* in the square formation, *Corners* stand across the corner of the square from each other (thus the name). The following persons are corners for each other: Lady 1 and Gent 2; Lady 2 and Gent 3; Lady 3 and Gent 4; Lady 4 and Gent 1.

A gent's left-hand lady is the same as his corner lady; and his right-hand lady is that lady in the couple to the right of, or in the couple ahead of him at a given time. From *Home Positions* the following are right-hand ladies for the gents designated: Lady 1 for Gent 4; Lady 2 for Gent 1; Lady 3 for Gent 2; and Lady 4 for Gent 3.

Dancers begin from *Home Positions*. They leave and return there from time to time when directed by the pattern of the "calls," and always return there at the end of each complete dance. Gents are called by names such as Gent 1 (2, 3, etc.), Head Gent, Paw, Boy, Dad, Crow. Ladies are identified by names such as Lady 2 (3, etc.), Side Lady, Taw, Girl, Mother, Mama, Sagehen, Sally, Dolly, Sue.

Dancers always use the smooth square dance step. It is a light, gliding walk without skips or jerks.

2 FORWARD AND BACK

Designated (active) dancers dance forward (four steps), and without pausing, dance backward to place (four steps).

"Heads go forward . . ."

CALL

Everybody*   *go forward and back*
Do it again on the same old track.

* Substitute *Gents, Ladies, Head Couples* (1 and 3), and *Side Couples* (2 and 4) for various uses of the movement.

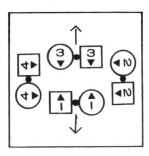

"Couples one and three forward and back . . ."

Note

When a Couple is active, the two join inside (adjacent) hands, the man's hand palm up, the lady's palm down.

3 CIRCLE: left, right, all the way, half
SINGLE CIRCLE: half, three quarters

To *Circle,* designated dancers step forward and join hands at about waist level (when genders are mixed, men's hands go palm up, ladies' palm down). Beginning on left feet, they step in unison and circle as directed. Circling left is clockwise (cw); circling right is counterclockwise (ccw). *Always* circle left unless otherwise directed.

For *Single Circle,* two facing dancers join both hands and circle left according to the call, half or three-quarters around, then wait for the next call.

"All join hands and circle left . . ."

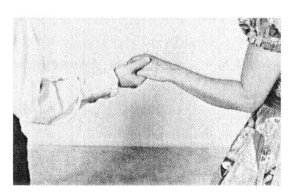

Position for joining hands.

CALL I

*All** join hands, *circle left* you know
All the way around and don't be slow

Now *circle* to the *right* as back you roam
Circle to the right 'til you get back home.

* Substitute *Ladies, Gents, Head Couples,* and *Side Couples,* for other uses of the movement.

Note

Designated dancers circle to the left (sixteen steps, around the circle), then circle to the right (sixteen more steps) back to home positions. Drop hands. It is important to stop exactly in home position after this call.

CALL II

Head Couples forward, *Opposites Single Circle*
Go half around and back up to opposite place

Side Couples forward, *Opposites Single Circle*
Go half around and back up to opposite place

All join hands, circle left around
Stop in place at your hometown.

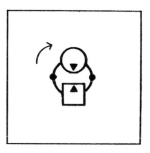

"Single circle half around . . ." Two facing dancers join hands and circle left half around.

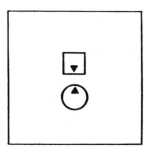

They stop facing each other from exchanged positions.

4 TURN BACK, (U-TURN BACK): single, couple

Designated dancers individually reverse the direction they face by turning left, or right, as determined by their position at the time of the call and the next movement called. When a couple is designated to turn back, dancers face toward each other during the turn. (See Movement 21 for a call using U-turn Back.)

"All join hands and circle left . . ."

CALL I

*All** circle to the left don't be slow
Circle to the left half around you go

Now *All** Turn Back, go single file
Return to place in Indian style.

*Substitute *Gents, Ladies, Head Couples, Side Couples* for other uses of the movement.

Note

All circle to the left eight steps, drop hands, make a *Right-face Turn Back,* and follow in order single file to home positions.

". . . all drop hands and turn back . . ."

CALL II

All *go* to the left, go single file
To the left around, go Indian style

Ladies (only) *Turn Back* on the outside track
Gents keep going, go clickety clack

Now *Gents Turn Back,* trail behind your own
Follow single file 'til you get back home.

Note

All dancers go left (clockwise) single file around the circle in consecutive order (eight steps). Ladies make a *Left-face* turn and go *Back* the other way (counterclockwise) around the outside of the gents, who continue moving clockwise. When partners are once again adjacent (eight steps), the gents make a left-face *Turn Back,* fall in behind their own partners, and follow them around the circle back to home positions (eight more steps).

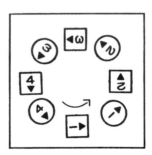

". . . all go to the right single file . . ."

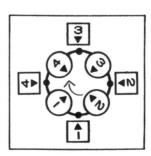

"Ladies join hands and circle left . . ."

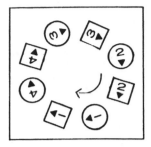

"All go left single file . . ."

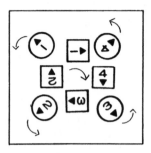

". . . ladies turn back on the outside track, gents keep going . . ."

". . . when she comes around, gents turn back behind your maid . . ."

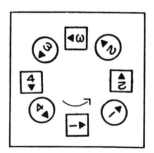

". . . all go to the right single file . . ."

5   BOW (HONOR)

Designated gent and lady face each other and bow (Honor) slightly at the waist. Inside hands may be joined. The lady may hold out her skirt at the side; the gent holds his arms near the sides of his body.

"Bow to your partner . . ."

CALL

Bow to (*honor*) your *Partners* then *Corners* all
Then *Bow* to *Opposite* girl across the hall.

6 SWING: waist (with, without twirl), two-hand

The square dance swing is performed in semiballroom (side-by-side) position by a gent and a lady. The designated gent and lady face each other and dance forward until standing right side to right side. The gent extends his right arm in front of the lady and places his right hand firmly around the left side of her waist. His left hand is extended sideward palm up, at a comfortable height for the lady to place her right hand across it palm down. Her left arm rests lightly on his right arm with her hand on his upper arm. Both pull gently against each other, and starting on left feet, *Walk* around in place (cw) side-by-side *Until the Gent Faces the Proper Direction for the Next Movement* (i.e. toward center if the movement to follow is to circle; counterclockwise, if the next movement is to promenade, etc.). He stops, releases the lady's right hand. She backs away to place at his right side. They change to appropriate hand positions for the next movement. (In some areas, and sometimes for exhibitions, a "buzz" step is substituted for the walk-around step. See "Steps and Figures" in the "Round Dancing" section.)

To add a *Twirl* at the end of a swing, when the gent faces the proper direction for the next movement, he stops. Then in one continuing, smooth motion, the joined hands (his left, her right) are raised in an arch (the gent firmly curving his fingers downward so the lady can steady herself as her hand lightly turns around them), and the gent guides the lady into a *Right-face Turn* under the arch. She takes two steps while turning. As the lady comes to position beside him, the gent shifts the lady's right hand from his left into his right hand to help stop her momentum.

For a *Two-hand Swing* (recommended for children instead of the waist swing), the boy and girl face each other, join hands (rights to lefts—boys palms up, girls down), circle left once around, and open to face proper direction.

Partners move forward to position with right sides adjacent.

They swing and walk around each other until the gent faces the proper direction for the next movement called.

". . . and give her a twirl . . ." Lady makes a right-face turn under her right and his left hands, which are raised in an arch.

Two-hand swing with gent's palms up, lady's down, and bent elbows held near the body.

They change hand positions. Gent takes lady's left hand in his right to stop her momentum.

CALL

All bow to *Partners,* then you *Swing*
Put ladies on the right and make a ring

Circle to the left and around you roam
Go all the way around 'til you get back home.

Note

Partners face, bow, and swing. When the gent faces center he stops and the lady backs to place at his right side in order to be in position to join hands to circle.

Important Note: When a gent swings a lady not his original partner, the new lady becomes his temporary partner, and her number designation temporarily becomes the same as his.

7 DO SA DO (dough-sah-dough) (DOCEY AROUND)

Designated dancers face and loop in a smooth continuous motion all the way around each other without changing directions faced. They move forward and to the left of each other, pass right shoulders, move to the right, pass by each other back-to-back, and back up to beginning place, passing left shoulders, ending face-to-face.

CALL

All face your *Partners,* do a *Do Sa Do*
Go all around your own just so

Face *Corners* now, *Do Sa Do* around
Back up to place in your own hometown

Heads (Sides) to the center and *Do Sa Do*
Go all the way around, back to place you go.

"Do sa do . . ."

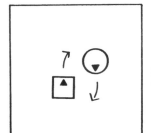

"Do sa do . . ." Two facing dancers sidestep left.

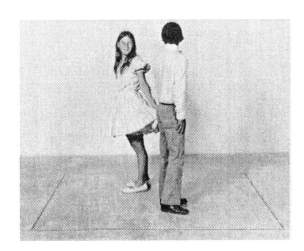

Pass back-to-back.

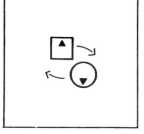

They pass right shoulders then back-to-back.

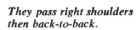

Pass left shoulders as they return to place.

Return to place.

8 MAKE A STAR: right hand, left hand

Designated dancers move toward each other and, staying in consecutive order, extend the hand indicated (right, left) palm out at shoulder height until hands touch lightly with fingers pointed upward. (In some areas gents use a "pack saddle" hand position. Each lightly grasps the wrist of the gent ahead of him.) Dancers stand sideways so that the shoulders and outstretched arms are like spokes in a wheel. The touching hands serve as the hub, and the dancers move forward immediately around the rim. A left-hand star turns counterclockwise; a right-hand star turns clockwise.

CALL

*All** to the center, *Make a Right-hand Star†*
Turn it around right where you are

Go all the way around, don't be slow
Dance full around, then home you go.

*Substitute *Ladies, Gents, Sides,* and *Heads* for practice in other uses of the movement.

†Substitute *Left-hand Star* for practice.

"Make a right-hand star . . ."

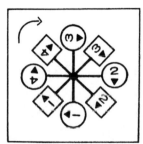

"All make a right-hand star . . ."

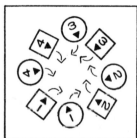

". . . all turn back . . ." or, *". . . back with the left . . ."*

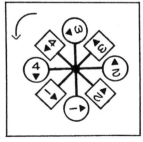

". . . to a left-hand star . . ."

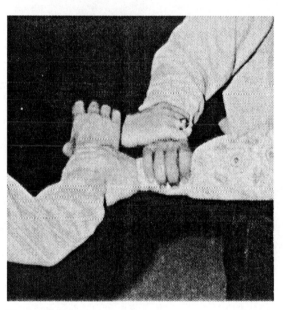

"Pack saddle" star.

9 BACK WITH THE LEFT CHANGE HANDS

Back With the Left is called when designated dancers are turning with right hands joined. Joined hands are dropped, dancers back out turning half right face, make a left-hand star, and immediately "turn the star" (ccw). (In some areas, when hands are dropped, everybody claps their hands.)

Change Hands means for two dancers who have a one-hand grasp with either hand to change to the other hand.

CALL

*All** to the center make a right-hand star
Turn it around right where you are

Back With the Left, don't be slow
Walk on around then home you go.

*Substitute *Gents, Ladies, Sides,* and *Heads* for practice in other uses of the movement.

10 LEAD TO THE RIGHT: couple, single

A designated single dancer, or a couple (with inside hands joined), dances diagonally toward the position at their right and turns slightly to the right into a place facing that position, or the person, or persons in that position. (See photos on page 26.)

CALL

Head (Side) Couples bow and then you swing
Lead right out *to the Right* of the ring

Now circle to the left with the couple you found
Head gents break, and leave these two, take your lady home with you.

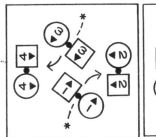
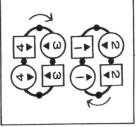

"*Heads lead to the right . . .*"

"*. . . circle four with the couple you found . . .*"

"*When half around, head gents break, leave those two, take your lady home . . .*"

Note

To return to home place smoothly after circling left, when the lead couple (head, side) is on the outside of the circle, the lead gent breaks hand holds with the lady on his left and goes to his home position pulling his partner into her place at his right side. When the couple visited have circled back to home positions, the lady in the lead couple breaks hand holds with the gent at her right, leaving that couple in original position.

11   CIRCLE (BREAK) TO A LINE

The active gent in a circle with two couples or more releases his left-hand grasp, then pulls the circle into a straight line facing into the square from the inactive dancers' position. To facilitate the movements, as the line straightens, the lady at the other end of the line ducks left face to place under an arch made by her left hand joined with the right hand of the gent at her left. (See photos on page 26.)

CALL

Head (Side) Couples lead to the right
Circle four with all your might

Head Gents break and *Make a Line*
Go forward and back you're doing fine

Circle eight to the left go all around
Stop in place in your hometown.

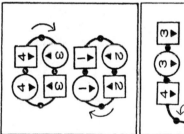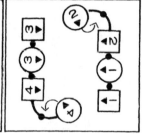

"Circle four with all your might . . ."   *". . . when half around, lead gents break . . ."*

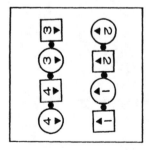

". . . to a line . . ."

12   BEND THE LINE

A line of an even number of dancers bends (breaks) in the middle (end dancers move forward, centers back up) into two short lines that wheel around separately to face each other about two steps apart. When two lines of four dancers *Bend* (break) *the Line,* each of the ends (couples) becomes part of another line. (See photos on page 26.)

CALL

Heads (Sides) lead to the right and circle to a line
Lead gents break you're doing fine

Dance foward and back in lines you do
Bend the line, face a brand-new two

New lines forward and back in time
Break in the middle and *bend the line*

Forward and back then eight join hands
Circle left to home around the land.

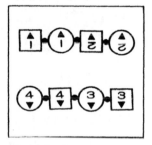

"Bend the line . . ."
(When four dancers are in a line.)

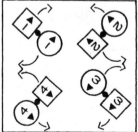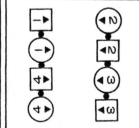

The lines divide into couples, then the partner on the outside of the line walks forward while the inside partner backs, moving around each other . . .   *. . . ending with new couples in lines perpendicular to the original lines.*

"Heads lead to the right . . ."

". . . to a line . . ."

". . . and circle . . ."

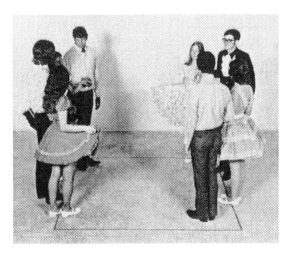

". . . and bend the line . . ."

Ladies duck under an arch to the line.

. . . ending in new lines of four perpendicular to the original lines.

13 STAR PROMENADE: reverse, mixed

In *Star Promenade,* two or more (usually four) gents, each with a lady at his right, turn a left-hand "pack saddle" star (each lightly grasps the left wrist of the gent in front of him) counterclockwise. Inside arms of couples are around each other's waists. (To "spread the star," ladies move away from waist holds to inside hand holds with gents.)

In *Reverse Star Promenade,* ladies make a right-hand star (regular, no pack saddle) with gents at their left sides.

In a *Mixed Star Promenade,* two ladies and two gents with partners at their right sides form the star promenade.

CALL

Gents to the center make a Left-hand star
Turn it around but not too far

Pick up your partners with a left arm around
Star Promenade back to your hometown

Ladies to the center make a Right-hand star
Turn it around but not too far

Pick up your partners with a left arm around
Reverse Star Promenade to your own hometown.

Note

When those turning in a star have gone full around, back to home position, the partner steps forward within arm's reach, and without slowing down, they put inside arms around each other's waists and continue moving in a star promenade.

"*Star promenade . . .*"

Ladies turn back from a star promenade.

"*Reverse star promenade . . .*"

14 INSIDE (back) OUT, OUTSIDE (go) IN (HUB BACKS OUT, RIM GOES IN)

This movement changes a *Star Promenade* into a *Reverse Star Promenade* or vice versa. Each couple wheels around in place as a unit; the inside persons drop hands in the center and back out as their partners dance forward to form the center of the star with their free hands. The star then turns forward in the opposite direction. (Sometimes dancers make an extra full turn around each other when reversing the star promenade.)

CALL

*Gents** to the center make a left-hand star*
Go all the way around right where you are

Pick up your partner with a right arm around*
Star promenade around the town

Inside (back) *out, outside* (go) *in*
Reverse directions and you're gone again

Inside back out, circle left you know
Circle to the left and home you go.

*Substitute *Ladies* making a right-hand star then picking up partners with a left arm around him for practice.

Note

Dancers continue turning in the star promenade until hearing the next call. In the last couplet of the call, the inside dancers back out to form a circle in order to circle left to home positions.

15 PROMENADE (PROMENO): half, three quarters, wrong way, inside, outside (couples) PROMENADE SINGLE FILE ROLL PROMENADE

The *Promenade* is danced counterclockwise (in the same direction as the left-hand star and star promenade) by designated couples, or singles, following each other in consecutive order from starting position around a circular pattern (sixteen steps for full promenade). For couple promenading, the *Standard Position* is side-by-side (lady at man's right). Both hands are clasped between and in front of the couple at the lady's waist level—right hand to right hand above left hand to left hand in crossed hand position. The gent's palms face up with the lady's palms facing down across them, all fingers pointing forward. (In some areas dancers use the Varsouvianna or skater's positions for promenading. See "Round Dance Positions.")

In *Promenade Halfway* around to opposite place, designated couples promenade "outside" (behind) the inactive couples (who move forward momentarily, then back). Some calls direct the active dancers to promenade "inside" (in front of) inactive couples.

Promenade Three Quarters calls for designated couples to dance three fourths of the way around the outside of the circle, stopping in the place of (or behind) the couple originally at their left.

Promenade Wrong Way is danced clockwise by couples in *Standard Position* (lady at gent's right and on the inside).

Roll Promenade is called when a gent and a lady have left hands joined, as in a left-hand

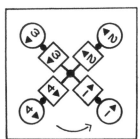

"Star promenade . . ."

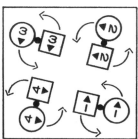

". . . inside out, outside in . . ."

"Reverse star promenade . . ."

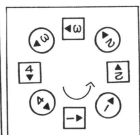

"Promenade single file, Indian style . . ."

"Promenade two-by-two . . ."

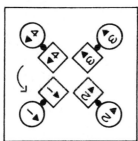

Promenade hand positions.

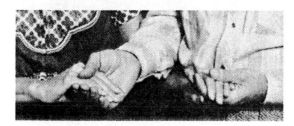

"Promenade two-by-two . . ."

"Heads promenade halfway around . . ." Sides move forward temporarily to allow them to pass.

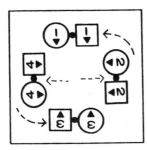

Heads have exchanged places.

swing (or an allemande thar, see movement 42), when the lady is facing counterclockwise (promenade direction) and the gent is facing clockwise (the opposite direction). The gent turns left face toward the lady without releasing left hands, ending in couple promenade position.

Single-file Promenade is danced by designated single dancers following each other in consecutive order from their starting positions around the circle counterclockwise (same direction as left-hand star).

CALL I

Each *Gent* bow and swing your maid
Put her on your right and *Promenade*

Promenade go around the town
With the right foot up and the left one down

Promenade one and promenade all
Promenade full around the hall.

Note

All four couples finish the swing facing counterclockwise around the circle and change to the proper hand position before promenading.

CALL II

Head* (Side) Couples Promenade Halfway Around
Around the *Outside** go then settle down

Same two forward circle left you know
Circle to the left, back home you go.

*Substitute *Heads,* then *Sides* promenading *Inside* the inactive couples for practice.

CALL III

All Four Ladies (Gents) Promenade Single File
Inside that big old ring

All the way around you go
Then give your guy (lady) a swing.

CALL IV

Ladies star right around the town
Swing partners all with your left around

Gents Roll Promenade as you come down
Promenade around to your hometown.

16 GRAND RIGHT AND LEFT
(without, with twirl)
WEAVE THE RING (variation)

All dancers face partners and lightly join right hands (like shaking hands). Gents will follow gents around the circle (ccw), and ladies will follow ladies (cw) around the circle, weaving in and out with each other and lightly joining every other hand with every other person, similar to alternately shaking right and left hands and "pulling by" (see "Pull-by," "The Special Language of Square Dancing: A Selected Glossary") each one, passing right shoulders, then left shoulders, until partners meet again (eight steps). (In some areas dancers hold hands pointing up at about shoulder height and use a palm-to-palm finger handclasp.)

To *Twirl* after the grand right and left and before promenading, when partners meet, the gent makes a high arch with his right arm and firmly curves the fingers downward to steady the lady as her hand slides around the fingers and she takes two steps while making a full right-face turn (twirl) under the arch before they change to proper hand position and promenade. The lady travels along beside the gent (ccw) while twirling in order not to stop his progress (also used to end a promenade).

Weave the Ring follows the same pattern as grand right and left, without joining hands in passing. Men hold free arms near sides; ladies hold skirts out at the sides.

CALL

Face your honey, *All Right and Left Grand**
Meet every other one with every other hand*

Right and left around 'til you meet your maid
Then join both hands and promenade

Promenade two and promenade four
Keep that calico off of the floor.

*Repeat substituting *Weave the Ring* for *Right and Left Grand* and "but don't touch hands" for "with every other hand."

Note

When partners meet with right hands on the other side of the square, they join left hands underneath the right hands in promenade position, and without stopping, the lady backs to gent's right side to promenade to home position.

"Grand right and left . . ." (beginning position).

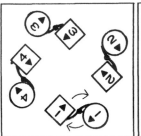

"Grand right and left . . ."

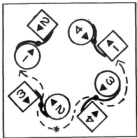

". . . meet every other one with every other hand . . ."

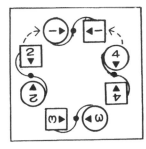

". . . 'til you meet your own again . . ."

**17 ARM (hand) SWING or TURN: right, left (half, three quarters, full around)
TURN THROUGH (includes pull-by): right, left
TURN BACK (after Grand Right and Left)
CATCH ALL EIGHT**

To *Arm Swing,* two dancers use the arm designated (right, left) as a pivot in swinging or turning around each other. A gentle *Forearm* grasp, with slight pressure, between the wrist and elbow, is used (even when "hand" is substituted for "arm" in the call), with the elbow bent at a forty-five-degree angle and firmly held close to the body near the lady's waist level. (Some dancers hold hands pointing up at about shoulder height and use a palm-to-palm handclasp.) For *Swing Half,* they swing until they have exchanged places. For *Swing Three Quarter,* they turn one quarter more. *Full Around* takes each back to place.

Turn Through is an *arm turn* followed by a pull-by, as in right and left grand, ending with dancers back-to-back facing the direction indicated by the next call.

Turn Back is usually called when partners meet with right hands after the grand right and left. They swing half around to reverse the directions faced. It is usually followed by a reverse or wrong way grand right and left.

In *Catch All Eight,* two active dancers swing half around by the right, change hands, and swing all the way around by the left arms. (See page 32 for Calls.)

Dancers swing each other around . . .

. . . until back to position . . .

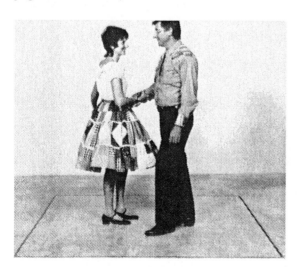

"Right turn through . . ." (beginning position).

. . . and pull by to end back-to-back.

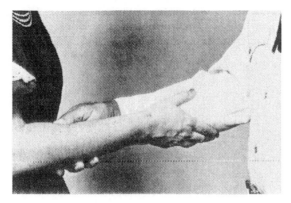

Forearm swing position for arm swings and turns.

18 FORWARD 1, 2 . . . (pull-bys)

In a grand right and left type of movement, when a line or circle is made up of facing pairs of dancers, the dancers begin with right-hand grasps, and weaving in and out, alternate right- and left-hand grasps as they meet and pull by the number of dancers called, ending past the last one. (See *"Pull-by,"* "The Special Language of Square Dancing: A Selected Glossary"; also Movement 16, Grand Right and Left.)

CALL I

Face Partners and *Turn* with a *Right Arm Swing*
Turn Corners with the *Left* at the side of the ring

Now partners right and around you go
Corners with the left and don't be slow

Meet your own in a right and left grand
Meet every other one with every other hand

Right and left go around the ring
Then promenade home with your own pretty thing.

Note

Arm swings are done with a forearm grasp; grand right and left with a handclasp, like shaking hands.

CALL II

Face partners and do sa do then *Catch All Eight*
Turn partner half by the right, change to left-hand swing

All the way around and roll promenade
Promenade home with your pretty maid.

CALL III

Heads (*Sides*) promenade halfway around
To center, *Turn Through* with the one you found

Face corner now do a left allemande
Back to partner and promenade around.

CALL

Bow to partner and take her right hand
Go forward now in the right and left grand

Go *Forward* four, left turn back
Go right and left back along the track

Do sa do your own, and promenade
Promenade home with your own maid.

19 ALLEMANDE LEFT
ALLEMANDE RIGHT

"Allemande left . . ."

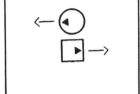

"Left turn through . . ."   *Pass left shoulders.*
or, "Allemande left . . ."

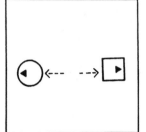

Ending back-to-back.

Allemande Left is a left arm Turn Through between corner dancers. (In modern dancing it is an *arm* turn, although traditionally called allemande left with your left *hand*.) If corner dancers are not already facing, each dancer turns to face his or her corner. With a left forearm grasp they swing half around to exchange places, release the grasp, then pass left shoulders by each other to a position with partners facing.

Allemande Right is a right arm Turn Through between a gent and his right-hand lady.

CALL

Allemande Left with your left hand (arm)
Go back to your partner for the right and left grand

Right and left 'til you meet your maid
Then take her by the hand and promenade

Promenade go one and all
Promenade your pretty girl around the hall

Promenade, go two by two
Promenade home like you always do.

20 PAIR OFF

Designated individual dancers turn backs to the center of the set. With all couples in home positions, the opposite couples designated step forward and each dancer turns away from partner to face his or her corner dancer; thus active dancers become partners with their opposites.

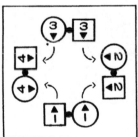

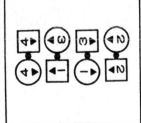

"Head couples pair off . . ." They dance forward and turn back-to-back . . .   *. . . ending facing corners.*

CALL

Head (Side) Couples forward and *Pair off*
Face the sides (heads) and do sa do

Allemande left with your left hand
Go back home and there you stand.

21 PASS THROUGH

Facing dancers pass right shoulders with the opposite, ending back-to-back.

"Pass through . . ."

Dancers pass right shoulders with opposites.

CALL

Head (Side) Couples forward and back with
    you
To the center again and *Pass Through*

Then U-turn back, your opposites face
Pass Through again, U-turn in home place.

22 SEPARATE

Two designated side-by-side dancers facing out of the square turn back-to-back, then dance away from each other and follow the next call. (See Movement 23, *Around One/Two*, to a line.)

CALL

Head (Side) Couples forward and pass through
Separate, go behind the sides you do

Gent to the left, lady to the right
Go back home if it takes all night.

Note

Dancers meeting on the outside of the ring should pass right shoulders.

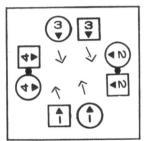

"Head couples move forward . . ."

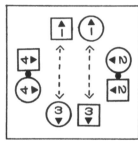

". . . pass through with the opposite two . . ."

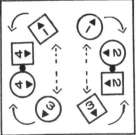

". . . then separate, gent go left, lady right . . ."

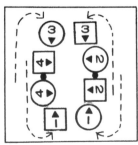

". . . go around the outside back to home . . ."

23 AROUND ONE/TWO: (to center)
(to a line)

A designated couple facing out of the square turns back-to-back and each goes around behind and to the other side of the nearest person (*Around One*) or persons (*Around Two*) on their other side, then follow the next call. Inactive dancers move aside momentarily, allowing active dancers to pass. If the next call is "to a line," active dancers stop in line with the person they have danced around.

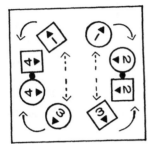

"... pass through ... then separate ..."

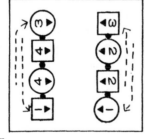

"... go around two and stop in a line."

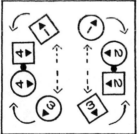

"Pass through ... then separate ..."

"... and go around one ..."

CALL I

Heads (*Sides*) dance to the middle and back with you
Now forward again and pass through

Separate, *Go Around Two*
Meet at home like you always do.

CALL II

Heads (*Sides*) up to the center and back with you
Forward again and pass on through

Separate now, dance around real fine
Go *Around Two* and stop in *a Line**

Forward eight and back in line
All circle to the left you're doing fine

Circle full around 'til you get back home
Stop in place and don't you roam.

   *Active dancers stop in a line with the inactive couples.

CALL III

Head (*Side*) *Couples* pass through
separate, *go 'round one* you do

Go into the center, pass through
Stop right there, U-turn back

Circle four in the middle of the floor
Back out to home as you were before.

Two facing couples move diagonally forward (right or left as called) as a unit to form a two-faced line, or if already in a line, to end back-to-back.

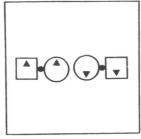

"... veer to the left ..."

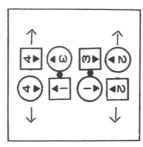

"... to a line ..."

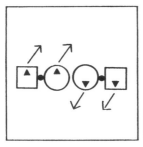

"... veer to the right ..."

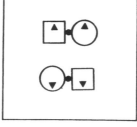

"... and face out ..."

CALL

Heads (Sides) to the center of the set
Veer left to a line, you're not through yet

Veer to the right, stand back-to-back
Promenade outside around the track

Promenade half around go two by two
Stop at home like you always do.

Two side-by-side dancers pass between two dancers facing them. The facing pair step away from each other momentarily, allowing the designated dancers to pass through.

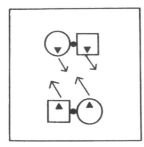

"Center two split the outside two ..." Outside couples move apart.

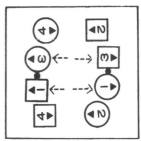

Allowing the center couples to go between them.

CALL

Head (Side) Couples pair off in the middle of the floor
Split Two at the sides (heads), dance a little more

Separate now, go around one
To a line of four, you're not done

Forward and back, then join eight hands
Circle to home, all around the land.

"Heads pair off ..." Partners step forward and turn backs to each other to face corners ...

"... and split the outside two ..."

"... and separate and around one ..."

"... to a line ..."

26 SQUARE THROUGH: two hands (half), three hands (three quarters), four hands (full), left

Square Through is danced by two facing couples (any combinations of men and/or women) and consists of a designated number of handclasps followed with pull-bys (similar to a small, four-person right and left grand) and precise quarter turns. (See illustrations pages 38–39.)

In *Square Through Two Hands,* facing couples pull by opposites with right hands, release hands, turn a quarter to face partners, pull by them with left hands, and release hands. This leaves partners back-to-back in opposite's places.

TWO HANDS

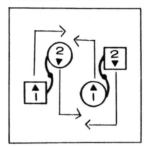

"Heads square through two hands . . ."

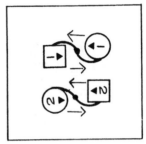

Partners pull by with left hands . . .

THREE HANDS

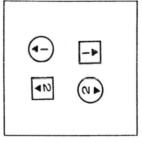

. . . ending back-to-back.

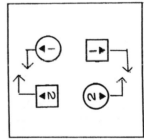

"... three hands." Dancers turn to face original opposites . . .

FOUR HANDS

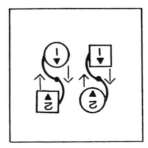

. . . then pull by with right hands . . .

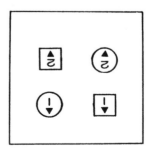

. . . ending back-to-back with opposites.

Illustrations for SQUARE THROUGH

For *Square Through Three (Hands) Quarters,* dancers continue movement above by turning another quarter to face original opposites and pull by with right hands; partners stop facing out from opposite sides of original places.

For *Square Through Four Hands,* dancers continue movements above and turn another quarter to face partners and pull by with left hands. Active partners are then standing back-to-back.

TWO HANDS

"Square through two hands . . ." Facing dancers join right hands and pull by . . .

FOUR HANDS

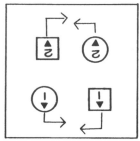 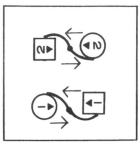

". . . four hands . . ." Dancers turn again to face partners . . .   *. . . pull by them . . .*

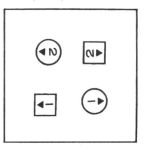

. . . ending back-to-back with partners.

. . . turn to partners, join left hands, and pull by . . .

Left Square Through movements begin by joining left hands with opposites and proceeding in opposite directions to those above, using opposite hands than those directed.

Any *Square Through* will have one less pivot (quarter turn) than the number of hands designated.

Note

Sides stand in place while heads do the square through ending in paired off positions facing corners.

. . . ending back-to-back with partners.

CALL

Head (Side) Couples do a *Full Square Through*
Count 'em as four hands you do

It's one, two, three, and four
Square through around the floor

There's corner now in front of you
So do sa do with the outside two

Right turn through on the corner of the hall
Go home and swing with partners all.

THREE HANDS

"... three hands ..." *Dancers turn again to face original opposites and join right hands ...*

... then pull by to end back-to-back with opposites.

FOUR HANDS

"... four hands ..." *Facing partners once again pull by with left hands ...*

... ending back-to-back with partners.

27 CALIFORNIA TWIRL (FRONTIER WHIRL)

A couple in standard position join inside hands, turn to face each other, and at the same time raise the joined hands in an arch, meanwhile letting the hands slide around, as the lady walks under the arch turning left face in front of the gent, and he walks around her (cw) until they are side-by-side facing in reverse direction.

"California twirl . . ." Couples join inside hands . . .

"California twirl . . ." Partners join inside hands, and face each other . . .

. . . then make an arch with the joined hands and the lady passes under the arch and to the right . . .

. . . make an arch under which the lady turns . . .

. . . while the gent moves around her until they are again side-by-side but facing opposite from the original direction.

CALL

Heads (*Sides*) pass through across the set
California Twirl, you're not through yet

Pass back through and home you go
California Twirl in place you know.

. . . while the gent moves around her, and they end again side-by-side facing opposite from the original direction.

Two facing couples, each with inside hands joined, move toward each other. The active couple *Dives Through* (goes under) as an arch made by the other couple moves over them. A couple facing out, away from the square at this point, automatically reverses the direction faced by doing a *California Twirl,* which leaves both couples facing in the same direction, one behind the other. The couples doing the *California Twirl* become inactive and stand in place until a movement including them is called. Those *Diving Through* remain active.

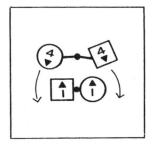

"Dive through . . ." The active couple goes under an arch made by a facing couple.

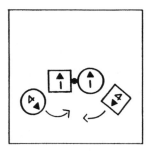

Facing couple moves the arch over as the active couple passes under it.

"Dive through . . ." The active couple goes under an arch made by a facing couple.

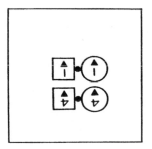

The arching couple does a California twirl to turn back to position trailing the active couple.

CALL

Heads (*Sides*) square through, four hands you go
Go full around, don't be slow

Face the sides, circle half around
Stop on the outside of the town.

Heads Dive Through, circle half in the center with the opposite two
Pass on through to the outside two

Allemande left on the corners of the hall
Go back home and swing you all.

A couple in standard position (lady at gent's right) does a counterclockwise wheel around to face the proper direction for the next movement. The gent holds his left hand palm up in front of his left side and puts his right hand around the lady's waist. The lady extends her left hand in front of the gent and places it palm down in his; her right hand is either placed palm out on her right hip to receive his right hand, or she uses it to hold her skirt out at the right side. The gent backs around, turning left face while the lady walks forward, turning around with him.

The function of the *Courtesy Turn* is to reverse the direction faced by a couple while keeping them in standard position with the lady at the gent's right side. *Courtesy Turn* is seldom named in a call, but is an understood part of Movements *30 Right and Left Through* and *31 Ladies Chain.* (See Illustrations.)

Two facing couples briefly clasp right hands with opposites (like shaking hands), then immediately do a right shoulder pass through followed by joining left hands and making a courtesy turn.

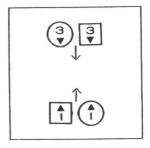

"Right and left through . . ." Facing couples move forward . . .

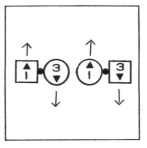

. . . momentarily clasp right hands of opposites, and pull by . . .

. . . while facing out they join left hands for a courtesy turn . . .

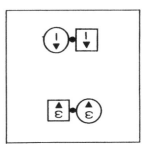

. . . then courtesy turn in place to again face their opposites, having exchanged places with them.

Heads (*Sides*) go forward and back with you
Forward again do a *Right and Left Through*

Turn the girls with an arm around
Now you're facing center of the town

Right and Left Through back the same old
    track
Partners turn in place when you get back.

"Right and left through . . ." Opposites join right hands and pull by, ending back-to-back.

Couples join left hands for a courtesy turn . . .

. . . and turn in place to again face the opposite couple, having exchanged places with them.

31 LADIES CHAIN: half, three quarters, two/four ladies GRAND CHAIN

Ladies Grand Chain is the same as 4 ladies right-hand star to the opposite, then courtesy turn.

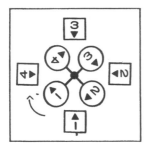

"Four ladies chain across . . ." Ladies right-hand star to opposite gents.

Opposite gents courtesy turn them . . .

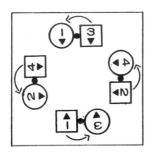

. . . to end in place with the new ladies as their partners.

For *Two Ladies Chain,* the two ladies in facing couples in standard position right-hand star to the opposite gent, who courtesy turns them to place as his partner (see Illustrations).

In *Ladies Chain Three Quarters,* either two or four ladies (side, head, all four) right-hand star to their corner gents (three quarters around the square), who courtesy turn them into place as their partners.

"Two ladies chain . . ." Ladies right-hand star to opposite gents.

Gents join left hands with them and courtesy turn them . . .

. . . to end in place with the new lady as his partner.

CALL

Head Ladies Chain across the square
Opposite gents courtesy turn 'em, keep 'em
    there

Side Ladies Chain across the town
Gents turn 'em now with an arm around

All Four Ladies Grand Chain Home
Gents turn your own, don't let 'em roam.

Note

After a lady chains, she temporarily dances
as a partner of the gent with whom she courtesy turned.

"Four ladies grand chain . . ." Ladies star across to opposite gents.

Opposite gents courtesy turn them . . .

. . . to end in place as their new partners.

32 WHEEL AROUND, standard, right-face
WHEEL ACROSS
DOUBLE WHEEL AROUND TWO (A COUPLE)

For a standard *Wheel Around,* designated side-by-side couples (any combination of ladies and/or gents) turn left face (ccw) side-by-side as a couple, the dancer on the left backing up and one on the right going forward, to reverse the direction faced. (For a right-face *Wheel Around,* designated couples turn right.) Retain the hand position when *Wheeling Around* from a promenade. Opposite couples who *Wheel Around* from a promenade will be face-to-face with the couple who had been behind them. They will also be in a line with the couple that was in front of them.

To *Wheel Across,* two couples in a line facing the same direction exchange places, at the same time reversing the direction faced. The couple on the left end steps forward and wheels half around to the right; the couple on the right end wheels half around to the left; both maneuver sideways to reform the line. *Wheel Across* from a two-faced line ends with the couples having traded places.

"*Wheel across . . .*" The right end couple in a line facing the same direction wheels left; the left end couple wheels right around them.

The couples move forward to each other's places, but reversing the direction faced.

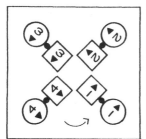

"*Head couples wheel around . . .*" with four couples promenading . . .

. . . each head couple reverses the direction faced by wheeling to the left . . .

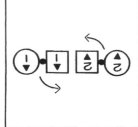

The couples reform the line from new positions.

"*Wheel across . . .*" from a two-faced line. Couples dance forward as in star promenade toward each other's places.

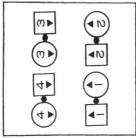

. . . to end facing the couple who was following them.

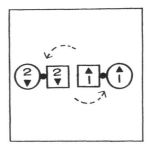

They stop in line when they have exchanged places.

For *Double Wheel Around Two (a Couple)*, all couples in a promenade (standard, star, reverse) keep moving during this movement. Designated opposites (heads, sides) make a complete 360-degree turn around as they turn out (right or left), around, and in behind the couple behind them who continue moving forward in the star, thus rejoining the promenade in back of the other couple. Danced twice, first by heads, then by sides, it puts dancers back in original positions; danced once, it gets two couples who are out of sequence back into place.

"*Heads* double *wheel around a couple . . .*" from a reverse star promenade.

As side couples continue the promenade, head couples leave the star, double wheel left around as those behind them pass by.

Heads rejoin the star behind side couples.

CALL I

Promenade one, promenade all
Promenade the pretty girls around the hall

Head (Side) two couples Wheel Around
Make two lines across the town

Forward and back and pass through
All California twirl and pass through

Sides California twirl and all promenade
Stop at home with your own maid.

CALL II

Heads (Sides) right and left through
Lead to the right, circle to a line

Lines Wheel Across and bend the line
Forward and back, you're doing fine

All join hands and circle left around
Go all the way to your hometown.

CALL III

All ladies star right around the town
Pick up partners with an arm around

Heads (Sides) Double Wheel Around just
Two
Rejoin the star now you're not through

Sides (Heads) now *Double Wheel Around
Two*
Courtesy turn at home like you always do.

CALL IV

Heads (Sides) right and left through
Then all promenade around you do

Heads (Sides) Double Wheel Around Two
Around a gent and a lady too

Promenade go two by two
Stop at home like you always do.

This is a coined name calling for individual movements of all eight dancers in a thirty-two-count routine that must be memorized. It is danced exactly in time to the music. In home positions, each dancer stands in a corner of one of four imaginary minisquares dividing the square area equally. Simultaneously, corner dancers start from opposite corners of the minisquare and dance four steps along each of the sides, turning on the fourth step; then reverse and retrace the route.

"Sides face for the Grand Square . . ."

Heads (*Sides*) begin by going forward toward center; sides (heads) by facing each other and backing toward the outside corner of the big square. There is less confusion if head and side couples are taught separately before attempting to dance *Grand Square* simultaneously.

Head Couples face center and dance forward (four steps); on the fourth step they turn to face partners (beside them) and back up to side positions (four steps); on the fourth step they turn to face opposites (now beside them) and back away to outside corners of the square (four steps); on the fourth step they turn to face partner and dance forward to meet them at home places (four steps) (do not turn). Immediately reverse direction, back away from

partners (four steps); turn to face opposites and dance forward to side positions (four steps); turn to face center and dance forward to meet partners (four steps); turn and back up to home positions (four steps).

Side Couples begin by facing partners and backing away (four steps); turn to face opposites and dance forward to meet them at the head places (four steps); turn to face center and dance forward (four steps); turn to face opposites (partners are now side-by-side) and back up to home positions. Immediately reverse direction, go forward to center (four steps); face partners, back away to head places (four steps); face opposites, back away to outside corner of the square (four steps); turn and dance forward to home positions.

Both *Heads* and *Sides* dance the *Grand Square* simultaneously, each starting at different positions. Each faces forward when moving toward the center or toward home position; and each backs up when moving away from center or home position.

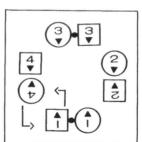

Position for Grand Square.

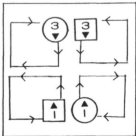

Heads' forward route (backward same as sides).

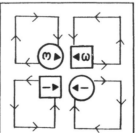

Heads back away from the center.

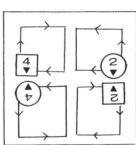

Sides' backward route.

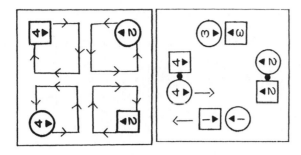

Sides go forward along the outside.　　*All reverse directions.*

CALL

Preliminary instructions before the thirty-two-beat section of music begins:

Sides face for the *Grand Square*, [then]

Walk 2-3-turn, walk 2-3-turn
Walk 2-3-turn, walk 2-3-reverse

Walk 2-3-turn, walk 2-3-turn
Walk 2-3-turn, walk 2-3-4.

34　DO PASO

Two or more couples simultaneously face partners and *Left Turn Through* (ccw); then face corners and *Right Turn Through* (cw); then *Courtesy Turn* partners in place (unless otherwise directed). This results in a series of interlocking figure eights made by each dancer with the ones next to him.

CALL

All join hands circle left you go
Break that circle with a *Do Paso*

Face partners and swing with the left arm
　　around
Then corner with the right arm as she comes
　　down

Now courtesy turn your own pretty maid
Take her by the hand and promenade.

35　ALL AROUND YOUR LEFT-HAND LADY

This is usually the first part of a two-part figure eight movement between corners and partners. The second half is explained in Movement 36. (The practice call and illustration are given with that movement.) Corners face and dance forward all the way around each other right shoulder to right shoulder, then pass by to position facing partners, as if doing a right turn through without joining hands.

36　SEE SAW

This is usually the second half of the preceding movement. Partners dance forward all the way around each other left shoulder to left shoulder, as if making a left turn through without joining hands, ending back to back. (In older calls, *See Saw* is a left shoulder do sa do ending with the dancers face to face.)

CALL

Men go *All Around Your Left-hand Lady*
See Saw your own little *taw*

Allemande left with your left hand
Back to your partner and there you stand.

Note
"*Men* go *All Around Your Left-hand Lady*, *See Saw* your own little *taw*" results in each person facing forward while following a figure eight pattern.

37 SASHAY (half)
RE SASHAY
LADIES TO CENTER, GENTS
SASHAY (left)
WHIRLAWAY (ROLLAWAY) TO
A HALF SASHAY

For *Sashay (half),* two side-by-side dancers facing the same or opposite directions move out of line momentarily and sidestep past each other to exchange places without changing directions faced. When facing the same direction, the gent passes behind as the lady at his right passes in front; when facing the opposite direction, dancers pass face to face. (When the gent's lady is at his left, they are in *Half Sashayed* position.)

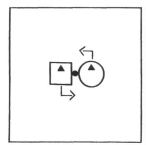

"Half sashay . . ." Starts with a couple in standard position.

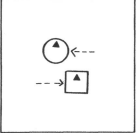

Ladies move forward and sidestep to the left, while gents move backward and sidestep to the right.

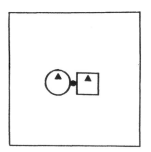

The lady backs up; and the gent steps forward to side-by-side positions.

To *Re Sashay* they reverse sidestep back to original places, with gent passing behind the lady.

For *Ladies to Center, Gents Sashay* (left), from a circle of eight moving left (cw), with hands joined, ladies release hands and move into the center temporarily as men keep circling. Ladies back out into the circle when the men who were on their right are on their left.

"All circle left . . ."

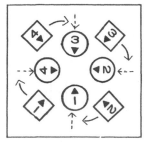

". . . ladies to the center . . ." (Gents keep circling left.) ". . . gents half sashay."

Ladies return to the circle at the gents' right side.

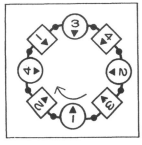

For *Whirlaway (Rollaway) to a Half Sashay,* a gent holding inside hands with a lady takes a step backward, gently guides her to face him, takes her other hand, and guides her to his other side as he steps into her place. If their inside arms are around each others' waists, he guides her to face him, then to place at his other side with arms around waists.

CALL I

Join your hands and circle the world
Gents Sashay Right around the girl

Now *Re Sashay*, go back to places
Circle left and tighten up the traces

Ladies to the Center, Men Left Sashay
Re Sashay, circle left that way

And home you go. . . .

CALL II

Heads (Sides) Rollaway with a Half Sashay
Pass through and turn back

Right and left through as home you go
Turn your girl in place you know.

"Roll away with a half sashay . . ." A couple is in
standard position with inside hands joined.

This is a grand right and left interrupted by
alternating do sa dos and sashays. Partners
face, do sa do all the way around, then join
right hands and pull by to the next one in the
grand right and left; facing dancers sashay all
the way around as if doing a left shoulder do
sa do (sometimes called seesaw), join left
hands, and pull by to the next; facing dancers
do sa do, join right hands, pull by; facing
dancers sashay, join left hands, and pull by to
face partners.

*The gent pulls the lady at his right around to face
him and takes her other hand . . .*

PRACTICE CALL

Allemande that corner, *All* do a *Grand Sashay
Do Sa Do,* look her in the eye, right hand pull
    by

Sashay the next one, left hand and then
Pull by *Do Sa Do,* I'll tell you when

Right hand pull by, *Sashay* the next one then
Left hand pull by, and swing the next one
    round

And promenade home. . . .

. . . and guides her to place at his left side.

Promenading couples turn toward each other, without releasing hands as they reverse the direction faced.

"Backtrack . . ." from standard position.

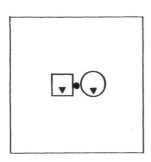

Without releasing handclasps, the dancers face toward each other as they reverse the direction faced and go clockwise with the lady at the gent's left side.

To *Box the Gnat,* a facing gent and lady, with right hands arched in a loose handshake grasp, exchange places (and directions faced). The lady then turns in a leftward movement and backs under the joined hands as the gent walks forward and makes a half-right-face turn. During the turn, the gent's hand slides over the lady's, ending with a handshake grasp and dancers facing from each other's original positions.

To *Swat the Flea,* left hands are joined and movements are reversed.

"Box the gnat . . ." A facing couple loosely join right hands and walk toward each other to exchange places. The lady turns left and backs under an arch made by the joined hands while the gent turns right face and walks around her . . .

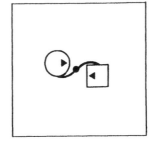

. . . ending facing from the opposite directions with hands still joined.

CALL

All promenade around the town
All Back Track as you come down

Go the other way around the track
Gents keep going *Girls* turn back

Meet your partner with a left-hand swing
Roll promenade around the ring

Home you go. . . .

CALL

Head (Side) two couples pass through
U turn back like you always do

Now *Box the Gnat** with opposites there
Stand face to face with that lady fair

Pair off then left allemande
Back to your own and there you stand.

*Repeat, substituting *Swat the Flea.*

"Box the gnat . . ." A facing couple loosely joins right hands and walks toward each other to exchange places.

. . . ending facing from the opposite directions with hands still joined.

The lady turns to the left and under an arch made by the joined hands while the gent turns right face and walks around her . . .

41 CROSS TRAIL
CROSS TRAIL THROUGH (Trail Through)
CRISS CROSS

For *Cross Trail* the person at the right side of a couple crosses to the left in front, as the person at the left side crosses behind them, ending with their having exchanged places.

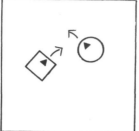

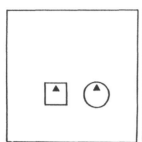

"Cross trail . . ." from a standard couple position.

The lady dances forward and crosses left in front of the gent who crosses right in back of her . . .

. . . ending on opposite sides of each other.

For *Cross Trail Through* (Trail Through), the above movement is preceded by a pass through of two facing couples.

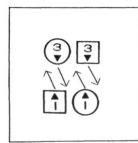

"Cross trail through . . ." One and three couples pass through.

Then the dancer on the right crosses in front of the dancer on the left.

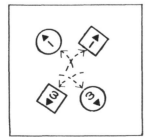

They finish after crossing, turned away from each other and on opposite sides.

For *Criss Cross,* an active couple splits an inactive couple facing them (who sidestep apart briefly to let them through, then close ranks) and cross trails to exchange places. Couples end back-to-back.

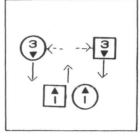

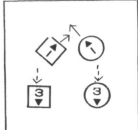

For "Criss Cross through . . ." Couple 1 splits Couple 3 as they move apart . . .

. . . then cross each other's trails . . .

. . . and end up on opposite sides of each other, while Couple 3 moves back together.

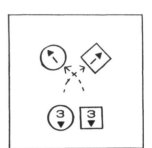

CALL I

Heads (*Sides*) right and left through
Turn your girls around you do

Then *Cross Trail Through*
To a left allemande

Left allemande with your corner maid
Go back home and promenade. . . .

CALL II

Heads right and left through
Pair off you do

Criss Cross through and separate
Go around one, pull by your mate

Allemande left with your left hand
Go back home and there you stand.

42 ALLEMANDE THAR STAR
WRONG WAY THAR STAR

After a left-arm swing between a gent and a lady, without releasing left hands, the gents make a right-hand pack saddle star in the middle and dance backward (ccw), as the ladies on the outside dance forward. (Inside dancers should take small steps so the ladies on the outside won't have to run.)

A *Wrong Way Thar Star* begins with a right-arm swing and is danced with the gent making a left-hand star and dancing backward (cw).

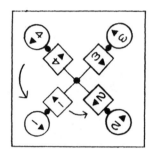

"Make an allemande thar . . ." with corners.

CALL

Partners left-hand swing like an *Allemande Thar*
Gents star in the center not too far

Back 'em up boys in a backward star
Ladies go forward right where you are

Roll promenade go around the town
With the right foot up and left foot down. . . .

43 SHOOT THE STAR

From an allemande thar star (or wrong-way thar star), the inside dancers break from the star formation, and couples left- (right-) arm swing into position for the next call, such as a grand right and left or swing the next or weave the ring, or turn back, or . . .

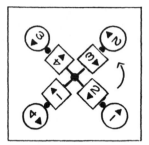

"Make an allemande thar . . ." with corners. Corners left-hand swing and retain hand hold as gents back up in a right-hand star.

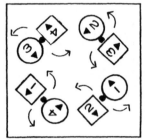

"Shoot the star . . ." from an allemande thar star. Couples break from the star and left-arm-swing to exchange positions.

CALL

Allemande left and allemande thar
Right and left (grand) and four men star

Back 'em up boys in an allemande thar
Then *Shoot The Star* right where you are

Right and left (grand) to the second pretty girl
Make a new star and make it whirl

Shoot The Star and find your own
Promenade that pretty girl home.

Note

In this call a grand right and left is interrupted twice (left-hand pull-bys are changed to left-forearm grasps) by a left-arm swing into an allemande thar star, then repeated after shooting the star. Gents make the first "thar star" with right-hand ladies and the second one with corner ladies.

44 SLIP THE CLUTCH (GEARS)
THROW IN THE CLUTCH

For *Slip the Clutch,* couples in an allemande thar star (or reverse thar star) release forearm grasps, ladies continue going forward, but gents stop backing and go forward in the opposite direction. All dance forward only to the next dancer, with whom they do an allemande left.

For *Throw in the Clutch,* dancers go full around to the same partner, or to the person designated by the call.

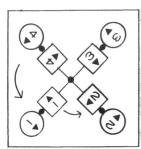

"... make an allemande thar ..." with corners.

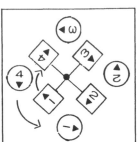

"... and slip the clutch ..." Partners release left hands, ladies keep going clockwise, and gents star counterclockwise to the next person (corner) for "allemande left ..."

"... and slip the clutch ..." Partners release left hands and all go forward to the next person (corners) for "Allemande left ..."

CALL

Partners left-arm swing to an allemande thar
Turn that star right where you are

Slip the Clutch to a left allemande
Right to your partner in the right and left grand

Right and left 'til you meet your maid
Take her by the hands and promenade.

"Allemande thar ..." Partners left-hand-swing to a thar star.

45 OCEAN WAVE: with, without balance

An *Ocean Wave* line is formed by three or more (usually four) dancers facing alternate directions with hands joined palm to palm, fingers up, at shoulder height. (Some areas use a forearm grasp.) Facing standard couples make an *Ocean Wave* line by stepping forward and separating slightly, so each lady can stand between the opposite couple, then all join hands.

To add the "balance," all dancers in the line take a short step forward with the left foot and touch the right toe beside it; then step backward on the right foot and touch the left toe beside it (step-touch, step-touch). ("Balance" is sometimes called "rock forward and back.")

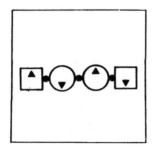

*Ocean wave formation.
A line of dancers face
alternating directions
with hands joined.*

*Ocean wave position. A line of dancers face
alternating directions with hands joined.*

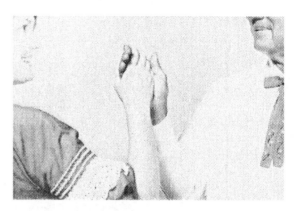

"Hands up" position.

*"Balance forward . . ." Dancers step forward on the
left foot and touch the right toe beside it.*

*"Balance back . . ." Dancers step backward on the
right foot and touch the left toe beside it.*

CALL

Heads (*Sides*) pair off, now do sa do
All the way around and a little bit more

Make an *Ocean Wave* and balance there
Balance forward and balance back

Pass on through and turn back
Box the gnat across the track

Change hands, do a left allemande
Back to place, there you stand.

46 ALAMO STYLE

An even number of dancers facing alternate directions in a circle with hands joined palm-to-palm, fingers up, at shoulder height, pause and balance (as described with Movement 45, *Ocean Wave*). (Some areas use a forearm grasp.)

"Allemande left Alamo style with a right to your partner and balance awhile . . ." Corners allemande left then without releasing handclasps join the right hand with partners and balance forward and back.

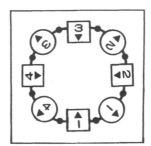

Alamo style position. Dancers face alternating directions around a circle.

CALL

All allemande left to an *Alamo Style*
Right to your partner and balance awhile

Balance forward and balance back
Turn with the right hand half about

Balance forward and back again
Turn with the left hand half again

Rock up and back again you go
Turn with the right on a heel and toe

Everybody balance up and back
Turn with the left on the same old track

Promenade one and promenade all
Promenade your pretty girl around the hall.

Note

In this case *Alamo Style* is done in connection with the grand right and left. It means simply that the allemande left (hand) grasp and the first right-hand grasp of the grand right and left are both retained while pausing to balance (with men facing in and ladies facing out). Then left hands are released and right hand grasps retained while dancers dance forward and rejoin left hands with the next person in the circle and hold for another balance (with men facing out and ladies facing in); and the same with each one met around the circle.

47 DOUBLE PASS THROUGH

Two couples face in the center, each with another couple following directly behind them (*Double Pass Through* position). The facing couples lead as each couple does a complete pass through (passing right shoulders) with each couple faced, ending with the trailing couples back-to-back in the center and the lead couples facing out in front of them (in *completed Double Pass Through* position). (See Illustrations on page 59.)

CALL

The call for this movement follows the next movement: *"First Go Left, Second Right."*

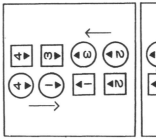 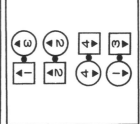

Double Pass Through with couples facing inward

. . . ends with couples facing out.

48 FIRST GO LEFT (RIGHT), SECOND RIGHT (LEFT): single, couples

For this movement, when one couple is following another, the first wheels to the left (or right), the second moves forward and wheels to the right (or left).

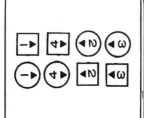

After head couples promenade three quarters around to position behind side couples, all "double pass through . . ."

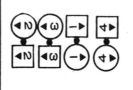

. . . to end with all couples facing out after passing through the couples faced.

The first (lead) couple wheels to the right, and the second (trailing) couple wheels to the left in "First couple right, second go left . . ."

Those two couples end facing a new couple and forming a line with each other.

CALL

Head Two (Side) Couples promenade around
Go three quarters around the town

Stop in place behind those two
Everybody do a *Double Pass Through*

First Couple Go Right, next *Go Left* around
Meet a new couple as you come down

Make lines of four with the couple at your side
Go forward and back on the old cowhide

All eight join hands in a circle you know
Circle to the left, back home you go.

"Double pass through . . ." Two couples face each other in the center, each trailed by another couple. (All move slightly left to allow space to pass.)

After double passing through, the center couples now face out, trailed by the same two couples.

". . . the first couple go left, second go right . . ." The lead couple wheels to the left, and the trailing couple wheels to the right.

A facing gent and lady, opposites, lightly clasp his right and her left hands in a palm-to-palm fingers-up position. With joined hands raised, the gent passes by the lady at his right and makes a quarter-right turn, as the lady walks under the joined hands and makes a quarter-left turn ending as new partners facing perpendicularly to the original direction.

"Star through . . ." A gent facing a lady takes her left hand in his right, and they make an arch. She turns to the left under the arch while he walks around her.

They end facing perpendicular to the original direction.

CALL

Heads (*Sides*) to the center and *Star Through*
Pass through, right and left through with the
    outside two

Dive through to center, *Star Through,* do sa do
Back up now its home you go.

In a line of four dancers facing the same direction and with hands joined, the two in the center make an arch. The ends fold (turn to face the center persons beside them, Movement 71) and join hands with each other to make a couple facing the arch. The new couple dives through the arch, letting go of the other couple. Those who made the arch automatically do a California twirl and fall in behind the other two, ending with all facing opposite to the original direction.

"Ends turn in . . ."
From a line with all
dancers facing the same
direction . . .

. . . dancers on the ends
of the line turn toward
an arch made by the
center two and pass
through the arch,
releasing hands as they
go through.

The arching couple
turns to follow them by
doing a California
twirl . . .

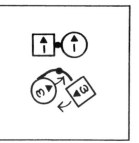

. . . ending with the
couples one behind the
other facing opposite
from the original
direction.

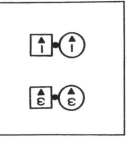

"Ends turn in . . ." from a line of four.

Both couples now face opposite to the original direction.

Inside couple arches as end dancers turn to face the arch and go under it.

The arching couple now trails those who were on the ends.

Ends form a couple after passing through the arch; the arching couple turns with a California twirl.

CALL

Heads (Sides) down the middle and pass
    through
Separate go round two

Stop right there, stand four in line
Forward and back you're doing fine

To the middle again and pass on through
The *Ends Turn in* and dive through

Star through in the middle you do
Side (Head) couples go right and left through.

51 SLIDE THROUGH

Facing couples, opposites, pass right shoulders. The gent always makes a quarter-right turn, and the lady always makes a quarter-left turn, ending in standard position facing perpendicularly to the original position and with their opposites as new partners.

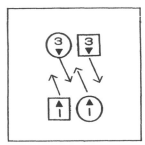

"Couples 1 and 3 slide through . . ." Facing couples pass through.

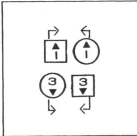

The gents turn one quarter to the right; ladies turn one quarter to the left.

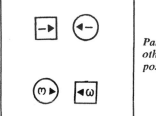

Partners end facing each other from a new position.

CALL

Heads right and left through across the set
Turn the ladies around you're not through yet

Slide Through go across the land
Pass through to a left allemande

Allemande left with corners all
Back to your own and swing you all.

52 CAST OFF: one quarter, half around, three quarters

From a line of four, center dancers separate, and the two end couples join inside hands (gent/lady, lady/gent, gent/gent, lady/lady). The couples wheel away from each other, with centers moving forward, ends backing to positions in accordance with the call.

Cast off one-quarter positions the couples back to back.

Cast off half-around positions them four in a line facing opposite to the original direction.

Cast off three quarters brings them face to face perpendicular to the original direction.

CALL I

Heads (Sides) to the right and circle to a line
Forward and back you're doing fine

Pass through with the opposite two
Cast off Half (around) you're not through

Right and left through across the hall
Turn your girl and promenade all.

CALL II

Head (Side) Ladies chain across you do
Head (Side) Two Couples pass on through

Separate around one to a line ["arky" position]
Forward and back you're doing fine

Cast off three quarters around you do
Then step forward and star through

First Couple left, *Second Couple* right and make two lines
Forward and back, you're doing fine

Allemande left with corners all
Then promenade partners around the hall.

"Cast off . . ."

". . . one half . . ."

". . . one quarter . . ."

". . . three quarters."

53 WHEEL AND DEAL: couples (side by side line) (two-faced line), partner

For *Wheel and Deal* from a line of four dancers facing the same direction (side-by-side line), the right-hand couple does a left-face (ccw) wheel-around to face the opposite direction, at the same time maneuvering to their right to a central position where the middle of their line was; simultaneously, the left-hand couple dances slightly forward and makes a right-face wheel-around and maneuvers left to position directly behind the other couple with all facing the same direction.

For *Wheel and Deal* from a two-faced line (couples facing opposite directions), each couple reverses the direction faced by wheeling toward the center of the line. They continue to turn forward, at the same time maneuvering slightly to the right, until facing the other couple.

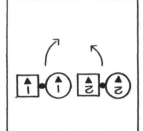

"Wheel and deal from a one-faced line . . ."

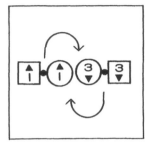

"Wheel and deal from a two-faced line . . ." Both couples wheel to the right toward the center of the line.

Right end couple wheels left to reverse the direction faced; left end couple wheels right.

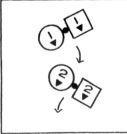

Left end couple falls in behind right end couple . . .

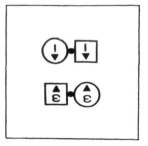

The couples maneuver to the right to end facing each other.

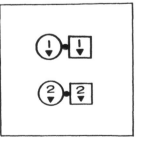

. . . ending one behind the other, facing opposite to the original direction.

For *Partners Wheel and Deal* the dancer on the right does a left-face turn (ccw) to face the opposite direction, while the dancer on the left does a right-face (cw) turn (fold) and stands in line behind the other.

CALL I

Head (Side) Couples to the right and circle to
  a line
Open it out you're doing fine

Dance forward and back then pass through
Now *Wheel and Deal* like you always do

Double pass through two by two
First couple left, and the next go right

Make two lines go forward and back
Circle to home on the same old track.

CALL II

Heads veer left to a two-faced line
Now *Wheel and Deal* you're doing fine

Right and left through across the town
Turn in place with an arm around.

"Wheel and deal from a one-faced line . . ."

*The couple on the right end wheels left to reverse
the direction faced; the couple on the left end wheels
right to fall in behind them . . .*

*. . . to end one behind the other facing opposite to
the original direction.*

Two facing standard couples join hands in a circle and dance exactly halfway around (couples exchange places), drop hands with the other couple, and each couple slides left to make a two-faced line (couples facing opposite directions).

Dancers face alternate directions with hands joined, as in ocean wave or Alamo style. First, "those who can" swing by the right (cw) (those with right hands joined), to exchange places and rejoin hands in the line formation; then "those who can" swing by the left (ccw) (those with left hands joined) to exchange places. Those who do not have the proper hands joined at a given time will stand in place.

Left Swing Through directs dancers with left hands joined to swing first, followed by those with right hands joined.

For a *Double Swing Through,* the complete movement is danced twice without stopping.

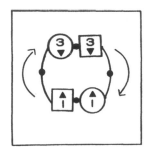

"Circle half around . . ."

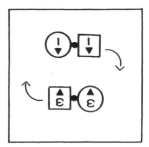

". . . veer left . . ."

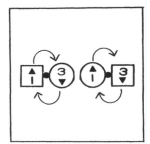

"Swing through . . ."
Those with right hands joined swing first to exchange places in the line.

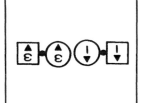

". . . to a two-faced line . . ."

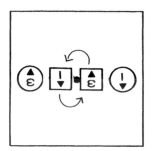

Then those with left hands joined swing by the left to exchange places in the line.

CALL

Heads (Sides) pair off face the outside two
Circle to a Two-Faced Line you do

Wheel and deal to face the other pair
Allemande left with your corner there

Back to Mama give her a swing
Stop in place at the side of the ring.

". . . and make a new ocean wave."

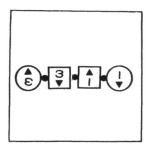

CALL

Heads (*Sides*) to the center, do sa do in time
All the way around make an ocean wave line
Swing Through, the length of the line
First by the right, then the left so fine
All step through and turn back
Right and left through across the track
Head Ladies chain across the hall
Courtesy turn at home, wait for the call.

Note

To step through from an ocean wave, dancers release hands and leave the line. Two dancers facing the same direction become partners.

Each dancer has exchanged place in line with the current partner.

Swing through: ". . . make an ocean wave line."

". . . then the left so fine . . ."

"Swing first by the right . . ."

. . . thereby forming a new ocean wave.

56 EIGHT CHAIN THROUGH: two hands and more

This is a right and left grand type of movement in which an exact number of pull-bys and courtesy turns are designated by the number of "hands" called (one, three . . .). To begin the *Eight Chain Through,* two standard couples are inside back-to-back facing *out* toward two standard couples on the outside facing *in.* (*Eight Chain Through* formation). In order to maintain the formation, when a couple has pulled by to a position facing *out* on the outside, instead of a left-hand pull-by, they courtesy turn and count it as one hand.

For *Eight Chain Through Two Hands,* the inside couples facing *out* pull by right hands with opposites (count one hand), then join left hands with each other and do a courtesy turn and face *in* (count two) to take the position of the outside couple; at the same time, the couples that were on the outside facing *in,* pull by right hands with their opposites (count one hand), then pull by left hands with the next couple they face (count two) and become inside couples facing *out* toward the new outside couples who are facing *in.*

For *Eight Chain Through Four Hands,* the two-hand movement is repeated (count one, two, three, four hands). For *Six Hands,* it is repeated twice (count one, two, three, four, five, six hands); and for *Eight Hands,* continue for eight hands.

For *Eight Chain Through Three Hands* (or any uneven number of "hands"), one more pull-by and courtesy turn is added to the even number preceding it (count one more hand).

CALL

Head (Side) two couples go forward and back
Pair off there, sharp as a tack

All Eight Chain Through a full eight hands
Count 'em boys go across the lands

Keep on going 'til you've done 'em all
Do sa do corners at the end of the hall

Allemande left with your corner man
Back to your own and there you stand.

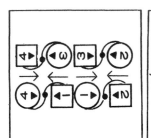

For "Eight chain through two hands . . ." the opposites of two facing couples first join right hands . . .

. . . then pull by. Couples facing out courtesy turn, and inside facing couples pull by again . . .

. . . ending with two couples facing each other again.

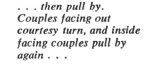

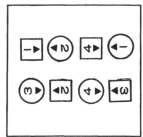

57 CIRCULATE: singles, couples, double
SPLIT (BOX) CIRCULATE

To *Circulate,* four single dancers or couples are in positions comparable to standing at the corners of a square box, all facing the same clockwise or counterclockwise direction. Designated dancers simultaneously move forward (cw or ccw) to take the place of, and face in the same direction (turning if necessary) as the dancer or dancers at the next box corner. Very often there is one box inside another facing opposite directions (see Illustration). Dancers in each box *Circulate* separately (i.e., parallel right-hand ocean wave lines have the four ladies in a center box facing ccw, while the four gents on the ends of the lines form an outside box facing cw).

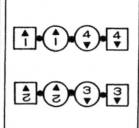

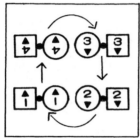

"Couples circulate . . ."
Each couple moves
forward around the
square.

They stop in the place
of the couple ahead of
them.

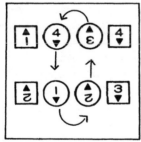

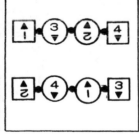

"Ladies circulate (from
an ocean wave) . . ."
Each lady dances
forward toward the lady
in front of her . . .

. . . ending up taking
that lady's place.

For *Split* (or *Box*) *Circulate,* there are two box formations side-by-side, and each circulates independently of the other.

Double *Circulate* means to dance forward two positions.

"Couples circulate . . ." Couples dance forward . . .

. . . to replace the couple ahead of them.

CALL I

All promenade, go around the town
Head (Side) two couples wheel around

Forward and back in lines of four
Sides (Heads) California twirl in the middle of
    the floor

All *Four Couples Circulate*
Ladies *Double Circulate* don't be late

Gents Double Circulate find your maid
All wheel around and promenade

Home you go.

CALL II

Heads (Sides) pair off you're doing fine
Do sa do to an ocean wave line

Ladies Circulate don't be slow
Gents Circulate don't you know

Ladies Circulate, all right turn through
To a left allemande, then back home with you.

For *Clover Leaf,* two couples facing out from opposite positions are each followed by an inside trailing couple (*Double Passed Through* position). The outside couple separates, and each dancer goes away one quarter around the outside of the square, trailed by the dancer behind him. Dancers meeting one quarter around become partners, face in, and dance forward, ending with new lead couples facing inside, and new trailing couples facing in behind them (double pass through position).

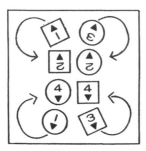

"Clover leaf . . ."
Couples facing out separate, go one quarter around the square, and face in and meet in the center.

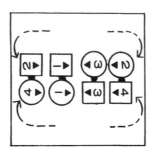

Trailing dancers follow and stop behind them.

For *Clover and . . . ,* from any formations with two opposite couples facing out, those facing out do a *Clover Leaf,* and the others dance the next movement called.

For *Clover Flo,* two facing inside couples are back-to-back with couples facing out (*Trade by* position, see Movement 67). Dancers facing out clover leaf then pass through; at the same time, those facing in first pass through, then clover leaf. This movement ends with dancers in an *Eight Chain Through* position (see Movement 56).

CALL I

Four ladies chain across, turn 'em around
Heads star through across the town

All double pass through and *Clover Leaf*
New head partners to center

Centers square through three hands around
There's corner now, left allemande

Back to your own
Promenade home.

CALL II

Heads (*Sides*) pair off, then right and left
    through
Pass through, then *Clover Flo*

Centers star through, outsides separate
Centers cross trail and skip one girl

There's corner now so left allemande,
Back to partners and promenade.

59 GO RED HOT

This is a promenade interrupted by a do paso type of movement involving arm swings between each gent and his right-hand lady (right arm), partner (left arm), and corner (right arm). To get into position, while promenading, partners release right hands, then gents guide their ladies across in front of them to face backward at their left sides. Gents are now facing toward right-hand ladies. They swing them with a right arm around; go back and swing partners left arm around; then swing corners right arm around; and return to partner with a left-arm swing to a roll promenade.

CALL

Promenade eight go around the town
All go *Red Hot,* don't slow down

Turn the right-hand lady, right arm around
Partner left, keep going around

A right-arm swing the corner maid
Back to your own and roll promenade.

One couple behind another facing the same direction exchange places. The couple in front makes an arch with inside hands and backs up, as the couple behind goes through the arch to become the active couple.

. . . ending with couples having changed places.

"Substitute . . ." The lead couple makes an arch with inside hands.

*The trailing couple   moves back over
comes under as the arch   them . . .*

CALL

Heads (*Sides*) star through in the center you
    do
Substitute, Sides (*Heads*) to center with you

Do sa do go around those two
Then *Substitute,* back over two

Centers star through then right and left
    through
Turn in place like you always do.

A lead couple exchanges places with a couple behind them, both couples ending facing original direction. The lead couple separates, each dancer turns away in a 360-degree turn, *Zoom,* around the person in back of him or her, as that person moves into the vacated place. A single dancer *Zooms* around a person in back of him or her. Back-to-back dancers will end face-to-face.

Couples (standard or mixed) meeting in single file do a miniright and left grand in a line. If couples begin from side-by-side positions, the dancer at the right steps in front and the other follows. Lead dancers pull by right hands, all four pull by the next dancers in line with left hands, those in the middle pull by right hands, ending in single file with all facing out.

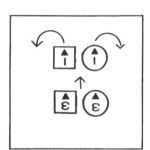

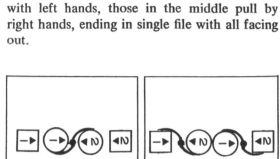

"Zoom . . ." The lead couple separates, and each turns back and goes around the dancer behind him.

"Ladies lead in a Dixie chain . . ." With couples in a single-file line, ladies pull by right hands . . .

. . . then left hands . . .

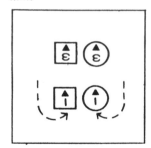

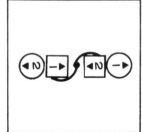   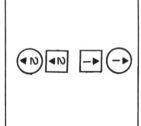

The trailing couple moves forward.

. . . then gents pull by right hands . . .

. . . ending with all dancers facing out.

CALL

Heads (*Sides*) star through in the center you do
Zoom, Sides (*Heads*) to center with you

Do sa do go around the two in front of you
Then *Zoom,* separate, go around the two in back of you

Centers star through then right and left through
Turn in place like you always do.

CALL

Heads (*Sides*) go forward and back the same
Ladies lead in a *Dixie Chain*

Ladies go right, *gents* left you go
All the way around to home you know.

63 DIXIE STYLE TO AN OCEAN WAVE

This movement is similar to an Alamo style right and left grand done by couples meeting in a single-file line as in the *Dixie Chain* (see Movement 62). Leads join right hands, pull by, join left hands with the next dancer, pull by, and hold on. The trailing dancer joins left hands with the lead dancer coming toward him, holds on, and joins right hands with the other trailing dancer. With all holding their handgrasps, each dancer makes a quarter turn to the left to form a left-hand ocean wave.

CALL

Side (*Head*) *Couple* go right and left through
Heads (*Sides*) *Dixie Chain to an Ocean Wave*

Balance forward, balance back
Swing through, go down the track

Turn through with your left hand
Do sa do right where you stand

Allemande left with corners all
Go back home for another call.

Note

Since this is a left-hand ocean wave, in the swing-through, the two in the center with right hands joined will turn first, then the outside dancers whose left hands have now been joined with the leads make their turn.

64 SPIN THE TOP

Four dancers face alternating directions in a right-hand ocean wave position. First, the ends right-arm swing to exchange places; then, simultaneously, new centers arm swing three quarters around (ccw) to a line perpendicular to the original line; and new ends move forward to place at the ends of the new line.

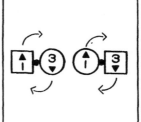 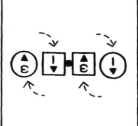

"Spin the top . . ."
From an ocean wave,
end couples swing right
half around . . .

. . . to a line.

 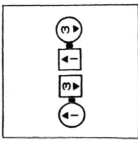

New centers swing left
three quarters around,
while ends continue
one quarter around . . .

. . . ending in a new
ocean wave
perpendicular to the
starting wave.

CALL

Head (*Side*) *Couples* promenade half around
    the square
Head Ladies chain, heads step to an ocean
    wave

Head Spin the Top now, and when you're
    through
Turn through, left allemande, go home to Sue.

When two dancers are side-by-side (facing the same or opposite directions), the designated dancer dances around to face the opposite direction at the other side of the inactive dancer. The inactive dancer moves sideways into the vacated place. For *Cross Run,* two dancers first cross trail then *Run* to each other's places.

"Gent run . . ." A lady steps forward momentarily then sideward, while the gent dances forward and around to her other side, changing the direction he faces . . .

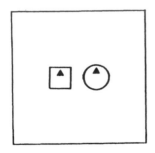

. . . ending with the gent on the other side of the lady.

CALL

Heads (Sides) pair off and step to a wave
Swing through, right then left, you're doing fine

Boys Run (Centers) around a maid
Wheel and deal don't be afraid

There's corner now, left allemande
Back to Mother and there you stand.

To *Trade* (places), two designated side-by-side dancers (or couples) exchange places, and in doing so, change the direction in which they were facing. If facing opposite directions at the start, they join inside arms and swing half around (couples star promenade half around), and end facing in the opposite direction.

For *Partner Trade,* two side-by-side dancers exchange places and reverse their direction by turning to face each other, passing right shoulders and turning to face opposite from the original direction. (For a standard couple this equals a California twirl done without joining hands.)

For *Couples Trade,* as a unit, side-by-side couples follow the same pattern as single dancers in partner trade.

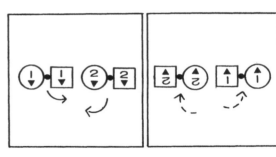

"Couples trade . . ." Two couples in a one-faced line wheel toward the center of the line.

The left end couple of the line passes outside of the right end couple to end up having exchanged places and changed the direction faced.

For *Ends Trade,* dancers at the end of any line move forward along the line to replace each other. They will be facing the opposite direction from the position in which they started.

For *Trade the Wave,* partners in an ocean wave (those facing in the same direction) step forward from the line and *Partner Trade* and reform the ocean wave, but now facing in opposite directions. (A right-hand ocean wave becomes a left-hand wave.)

"Partners trade . . ." Partners turn to face each other.

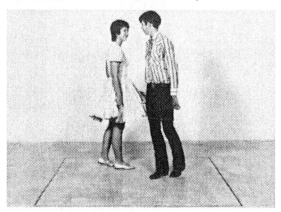

Pass right shoulders.

Turn to face back . . .

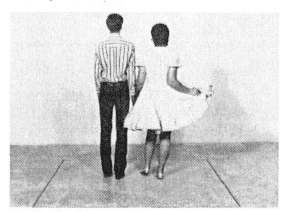

. . . ending having traded places and reversed the direction faced.

CALL I

Heads (Sides) forward and back you go
Step to center make a wave just so

End dancers Trade and all step through
Courtesy turn right there you do

Chain the ladies, across the hall
Turn 'em now in places all.

CALL II

Heads (Sides) pass through across the set
Partners Trade you're not through yet

Right and left through, go back home
Turn your girl, don't you roam.

CALL III

Heads (Sides) right and left through
Courtesy turn so true

Lead to the right, circle to a line
Forward and back, keep in time

Couples Trade, lines face out
Bend the line, all circle about

Circle back to place.

CALL IV

Heads go forward and back with you
Now step to a wave you do

Couple One Trade the Wave
Balance forward and back

Couple Two Trade the Wave
Balance up and back

Step through to your hometown
California twirl those girls around.

67 TRADE BY

With two inside couples facing in the center, each back-to-back with a couple facing out (*Trade By* position), the two inside couples pass through, while simultaneously, the outside partners trade and face in. This movement ends in the *Eight Chain Through* position.

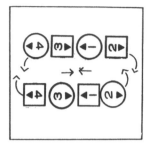

"Trade by . . ." With two couples facing in the center and standing back-to-back with couples facing out, the inside couples pass through while the outside couples trade . . .

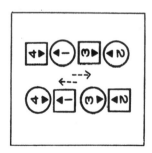

. . . ending with two couples facing each other.

CALL

Side (*Head*) *Couples* pass on through
Then *Head* (*Side*) *Couples* star through

All Trade by now and look out, man
There's your corner left allemande

A left-hand swing go around with you
Back to your own and promenade Sue.

68 FLUTTERWHEEL: two couples, four couples, reverse

With two couples facing, the dancer at the right goes to the center and makes a full right-hand turn, picking up the opposite inactive dancer as they pass, by joining left hands with their right hands and returning to place with them at their left side.

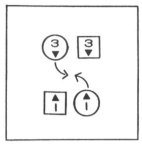

"Flutterwheel . . ." The ladies in two facing couples step forward.

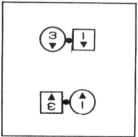

. . . star by the right to opposite gents . . .

. . . join left hands with the gents' right hands . . .

Take the new partners back to starting position . . .

For *Four Ladies Flutterwheel*, from home positions, four ladies star right to the opposite gents, join left hands with gents' right hands, and return to place with them as partners.

For *Reverse Flutterwheel*, the dancers at the left make a left-hand turn and pick up the opposites by joining right hands with their left hands.

CALL

Head (*Side*) *Ladies* chain across the set
Heads (*Sides*) right and left through

Head (*Side*) *Ladies Flutterwheel* across
Pick up opposite go home that way.

"Flutterwheel . . ." Ladies step forward . . .

. . . then star right to the opposite gent . . .

. . . and take him back to ladies' starting position.

69 SWEEP A QUARTER

Two couples who are turning while in a two-faced line formation with hands joined (as in *Flutterwheel*, illustrations 268–71), continue the forward movement one quarter more around the square before breaking from the other couple and maneuvering to face each other.

To add ". . . and sweep a quarter . . ." the couples continue turning forward one quarter more around the square . . .

. . . to end up perpendicular to starting positions.

CALL

*Head (Side) Ladies Flutterwheel across the set
Sweep a Quarter,* you're not through yet

Pass through, left allemande
Go back home and there you stand.

70 AND A QUARTER MORE

From any appropriate movement in progress, designated dancers continue turning in the same direction for an additional one-quarter turn.

CALL

California twirl face out all four
Partner trade and a *Quarter More* (face partners)

Right turn through to a left allemande
Back to partner there you stand.

Of two side-by-side dancers facing the same direction, the one designated dances forward and *Folds* (turns back) to face the other. If the two dancers face opposite directions, one *Folds* behind the other so both face the same direction.

"Lady folds . . ." The lady moves forward and turns to face her partner . . .

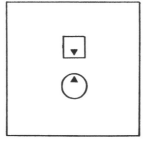

. . . ending with partners facing.

For *Ends Fold,* each dancer at the end of a line of four *Folds* toward the center to face the inside dancer beside him or her.

Cross Fold directs dancers to cross trail before folding (turning back).

CALL

Heads (Sides) pass through real fine
Separate around two to a line

Forward now then back with you
Ends Fold and face center two

Allemande that corner girl
Go back home and swing and whirl.

"Lady folds . . ." The lady moves forward and turns to face her partner . . .

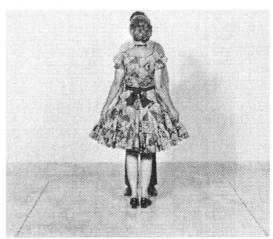

. . . ending with partners facing.

72 FACE/IN/OUT/TO THE MIDDLE: left, right QUARTER IN/OUT

Designated dancers turn individually to the left or right (one quarter) to change the direction faced as directed.

To *Face to the Middle* or *Face in,* dancers face the center of the square; to *Face out,* they turn their backs to the center of the square.

To *Quarter in,* partners turn to face each other; to *Quarter out,* partners turn backs to each other.

CALL

Heads (Sides) do sa do the lady across the ring
All Quarter in, do sa do (your own), and swing.

Dancers in a line turn to face the center of the line, all dancers step slightly to the left, pass (right shoulders) completely by those facing the other direction, and wait for the next call (face left, right, in, out).

For *Half Tag the Line,* dancers stop when adjacent to the other half of the line.

Partner Tag calls for partners to face each other, pass right shoulders, and wait for the next call.

Tag the line. With four dancers in a one-faced line . . .

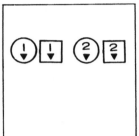

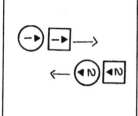

"Tag the line . . ."
. . . with four dancers in a one-faced line.

The two dancers on each end of the line turn to face center of the line . . .

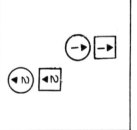

. . . then dance forward, stopping in line after passing by the other two.

The two dancers on each end of the line turn and face the center of the line . . .

CALL

Heads (*Sides*) right and left through
Turn the girls you do

Heads (*Sides*) to the right, circle left so fine
Head Gents break and you make a line

Now forward and back step in time
Then *everybody* turn and *Tag the line*

All face in you're doing great
Allemande left then promenade eight

Home you go.

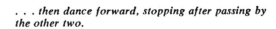

. . . then dance forward, stopping after passing by the other two.

With one couple trailing another, for *Center(s)* *In,* the center (trailing) couple in the set squeezes *in* between the couple in front of them (as they divide to make room). For *Center(s)* *Out,* making a line of four, the center couple divides and moves to the ends of a line, with the lead couple between them.

Outside(s) *In* directs the outside couple to squeeze in, and *Outside(s)* *Out* directs the outside couple to divide and form the ends of the line.

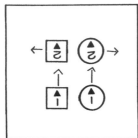 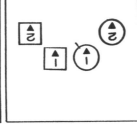

"Centers (couple one) In . . ." The couple facing out from the outside of the square steps apart . . .

. . . allowing the trailing couple in the center of the square to squeeze in between them . . .

. . . ending in a line with them.

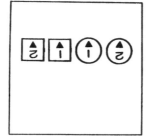

CALL

Four *Ladies* chain across you do
Heads star through, *All* double pass through

Centers In (leads separate, trailers squeeze in)
Cast off three quarters, 'til you face again

Star through and *Centers* pass through
Allemande left then home with you.

This is danced by a designated couple and equals a star through and girls turn back. A facing lady and gent take right-hand star hand positions, the gent walks by the lady and turns to face to his right; the lady backs under the joined hands in a three-quarter left-face (cw) turn, ending with right sides adjacent, facing opposite direction.

"Curlique . . ." A facing couple join right hands and make an arch.

The gent walks around the lady, turning one quarter to the right; the lady turns left as she backs under the arch three quarters around . . .

. . . ending side-by-side facing opposite directions and perpendicular to the original directions faced.

CALL

Heads (*Sides*) to the center and *Curlique*
Boys run around you know who

Allemande left with your left hand
Back to place and there you stand.

"Curlique . . ." A facing couple join right hands and make an arch.

The gent walks around the lady, turning one quarter to the right; the lady turns left as she backs under the arch three quarters around.

Ending side-by-side facing opposite directions and perpendicular to the original directions faced.

When two dancers in a single-file line are beside two dancers facing the opposite direction in a single-file line, simultaneously each dancer moves one place without changing the direction faced. Lead dancers move sideways (dodge) to the position at their right, while trailing dancers are going forward one place.

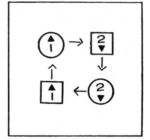

"Walk and dodge . . ." When four dancers stand in two columns, the dancers facing out sidestep to the right, while the dancers facing in walk forward to take the vacated place.

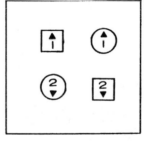

. . . ending with each dancer still facing the same direction but from a different position.

CALL

Heads (Sides) square through go full around
Everybody Curlique with the one you found

All Walk and Dodge then partners trade
Two Ladies chain, Men turn that maid

All slide through, then left allemande
To the old home place and there you stand.

Danced by two center couples back-to-back, each face an outside couple, or dancers in parallel ocean wave lines. Outside couples (those facing in) *Pass* (through) *to the Center* positions to become new facing inside couples (Those in ocean wave lines step through), while those now facing out automatically do a partner trade.

With one couple trailing another, the lead couple separates, and each dancer turns away and around to face the opposite direction forming the ends of a line. The trailing couple moves between the ends, and each separately turns back (facing away from partners while turning) to become centers of the line, all facing opposite from the original direction. (Dancers on the left turn toward the left; those on the right turn toward the right.)

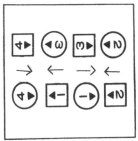 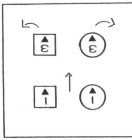

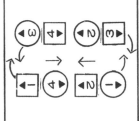 

*"Pass to the center . . ."
When two outside couples are facing two inside couples, they pass through.*

Then the new outside couples trade and face back in . . .

"Peel off . . ." The lead couple facing out separates and turns back . . .

. . . while the trailing couple moves forward and squeezes in between them, separates, and turns back . . .

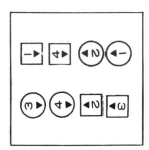

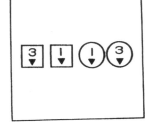

. . . into line with them facing opposite from the original direction.

. . . ending with all four couples facing in with one couple behind another.

CALL

Heads right and left through, all promenade
Heads (*Sides*) wheel around, make two lines

Lines go forward and back
All pair off (turn backs to center)

Peel off now, stand in a line
Pass through, turn back, and circle to place.

CALL

Four *Ladies* chain across the way
Heads (*Sides*) pair off face sides that way

Pass to the Center
New centers pass through

There's corner now so left allemande
Back to Mama, promenade the land.

Note

Pairing off from facing lines results in all facing out, one couple behind the other, lead couples in standard position (gent with lady at his right), trailing couples with the lady at the gent's left side. *Peel Off* puts all ladies at gents' left. Pass through and turn back put all into standard positions and consecutive order.

79 SPIN CHAIN THROUGH

This movement is an extension of *Spin the Top*. With dancers in parallel ocean wave lines, the ends arm swing to each other's places, new centers of each ocean wave arm swing three quarters around to form a new ocean wave across the set, perpendicular to the original line. Centers of this new ocean wave exchange places with an arm swing; then the new ends of it arm turn three quarters to reform parallel ocean waves with the lone dancers waiting there.

Spin chain through starting position.

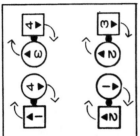 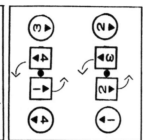

"Spin chain through . . ." From two parallel ocean waves, those with right hands joined swing half around.

Then centers (those with left hands joined) swing three quarters around to make a line perpendicular to the original lines.

Spin chain through "H" formation.

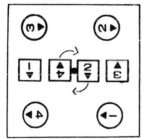 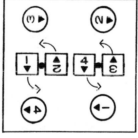

Those with right hands joined (centers) swing half around.

End couples then swing left hand around three quarters . . .

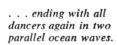 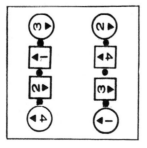

. . . ending with all dancers again in two parallel ocean waves.

Spin chain through final position.

CALL

Sides (Heads) flutterwheel across the land
Heads (Sides) square through four hands

Step to a wave, *All Spin Chain Through*
Spin and chain 'til you're back in line

Boys run, wheel, and deal around
Allemande left, promenade to hometown.

For *Partners Hinge,* dancers turn to face each other, then step forward and join right hands facing opposite directions in a line perpendicular to the original position.

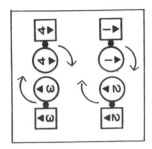

"Hinge and trade . . ." With couples in two-faced lines with side couples, all dancers move forward.

"Partner hinge . . ." A standard couple turn to face toward each other . . .

. . . then step forward and join right hands.

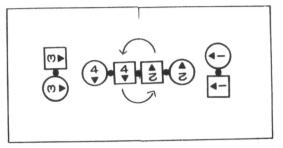

The couples facing out wheel to the right and maneuver left to the center of the line. The couples facing in wheel to the right and stop in

a perpendicular line with each other, join inside hands to make a line, and star promenade to exchange places.

For *Couples Hinge,* two standard couples facing the same direction in a line follow the same procedure. The couple on the left end wheels right, the couple on the right end wheels left, and both maneuver (veer) left to form a two-faced line perpendicular to the original line.

For *Hinge and Trade,* from parallel two-faced lines, the couples facing out wheel to the right half around to become an outside couple facing in (maneuvering or veering left to the approximate center of the original line); the couples facing in move to the center, men join left forearms, and couples turn (as in star promenade) until their line is perpendicular to the new outside couples; then the men release their grasp and the couples wheel left (and veer slightly left) to face each other, becoming center couples in front of the outside couples, ending in *Double Pass Through* formation.

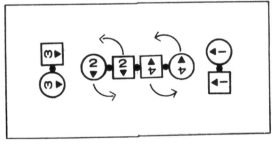

When again in a perpendicular line, each

couple does a pivot turn in place . . .

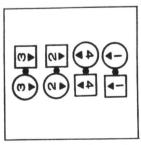

. . . ending facing each other in front of the outside couples.

CALL I

Heads (Side) Partner Hinge
Right turn through to corner men

Allemande left around you go
Stop at home don't be slow.

CALL II

Heads go right, circle to a line
Couples Hinge, make one long line

Wheel and deal, go right and left through
Allemande left and promenade home.

CALL III

Heads to the right, veer left to a line
All Hinge and Trade, you're doing fine

Centers chain those ladies so fair
Then pass through to corners there

Allemande left with your left hand
Back to Mother, there you stand.

81 SCOOT BACK

From parallel ocean wave lines, those facing in (scooters) dance forward and with inside arms turn through with the dancer coming from the opposite line; at the same time, those facing out fold into the place vacated by the scooters; scooters rejoin their own wave in the place vacated by those who folded. Ends and centers of the ocean wave have now exchanged places and reversed the directions faced.

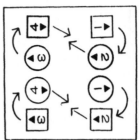

"Scoot back . . ." From two parallel ocean waves, dancers facing in move diagonally to meet opposites; dancers facing out fold into vacated places.

Dancers who are now in center turn through with the one they meet and then move into the place vacated by the outside facing dancers . . .

. . . ending with each dancer having exchanged places with the person beside him.

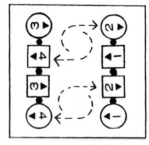

CALL

Heads square through, a full four hands
Do sa do to waves across the land

Scoot Back (those facing in turn through and
face out, others fold and face in)

From your new ocean wave *Scoot Back* again
Turn through with your right hand

Swing your Ladies around the hall
Wait right there for another call.

Note

Directional instructions within parentheses are "talked," to help dancers through complicated movements.

82 FAN THE TOP

For *Fan the Top,* with dancers in ocean waves or two-faced lines, the centers left swing three quarters, while the ends move up one quarter to end positions of the same line formation, which is now perpendicular to the original.

"Fan the top . . ." From an ocean wave, center, dancers left-hand-swing three quarters around, while the end dancers move forward one quarter around . . .

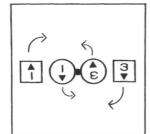

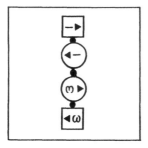

. . . ending in an ocean wave perpendicular to the starting formation.

CALL I

Heads (*Sides*) step to an ocean wave line
Fan the Top, you're doing fine

(*Centers* left swing three quarters, *Ends* move
    up a quarter to the
end of the line, make new ocean waves)

Now *Fan the Top* again
Centers left swing three quarters, *Ends* move
    up a quarter, make a new line

Cross trail through to a left allemande
Go back home and there you stand.

83 TURN AND LEFT THROUGH TURN THROUGH AND PARTNER TRADE

For *Turn and Left Through,* two mixed facing couples (ladies at gents' left), *Turn Through* with opposites (see Movement 17) (original couples will have changed sides and will be facing out), then courtesy turn to face the other couple again.

CALL

Heads (*Sides*) roll away with a half sashay
Heads (*Sides*) *Turn and Left Through** across
    the way.

*Repeat, substituting *Turn Through and Partners Trade.*

This is an interrupted right and left grand type of figure, with turn throughs (also called turn back) at intervals. Partners face and go forward two, then back one; forward two, then back one; repeating this sequence until they meet each other again. Partners right hand pull-by, left hand turn through the next (gent's right hand lady), go back and right turn through with partner; then left pull-by the next (right hand lady), right turn through the next (opposite), left turn through (right hand lady); and repeat to get back to partners.

CALL

Allemande left to a *Daisy Chain*
Go forward two turn back one

Turn her by the right
Go forward two with a left and a right

Turn back one with a left hand around
Go forward two, right and a left

Turn back with the right hand around
Go forward two with a left and a right

Turn back with the right
To a left allemande

Meet your own and promenade home.

All four dancers in a right-hand ocean wave release hands, and each gent reaches across in front of the lady at his right to take her left hand in his right. Without joining the free hands, each couple circles left (until the gent has reversed the direction faced) to a two-person line facing the couple from the other end of the ocean wave. (In a variation, hands are not joined. The lady folds behind the gent at her right and gents crossfold, as each lady follows the gent into position as his partner facing the other couple.)

"Recycle . . ." From an ocean wave, end dancers reach across with right hands in front of the person at their right and take their left hand.   *They pull that person into place as a partner at their right side.*

 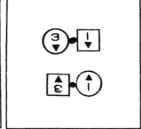

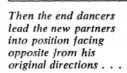

Then the end dancers lead the new partners into position facing opposite from his original directions . . .   *. . . ending with the two couples facing each other.*

CALL

Heads pair off and step to a wave
All Recycle around so two face two

Right and left through across the set
Two Ladies chain you're not through yet

Allemande left with your left hand
Back to partner, there you stand.

Selected Square Dance Calls

Calls given here (with a few marked exceptions) are representative of modern square dancing as it is practiced today. They include patter calls, singing calls, and calls for openings, breaks, endings, and fill-in patter.

The patter calls are copied with permission from recordings on the Blue Star label by Marshall Flippo. They may be called to any square dance music accompaniment.

Each singing call is set to a particular tune, and goes by the name of the title. Singing calls included here are classic examples of earlier dances (some with later versions) that have been widely danced. Since singing calls are constantly being choreographed to accompany new tunes, other current selections are not included.

Special square dance records (mostly 45 rpm) for patter calls (usually hoedowns) and for singing calls (called on one side, instrumental only on the other, with printed cue sheets) are available from markets listed in periodicals named in the Bibliography.

The patter calls given here include the introduction and figure (ending must be selected and added for dancing). The calls are divided into two groups, and for reference are numbered and the grouping is indicated. The first group is limited to selections from the easier Movements 1–50 and are marked, e.g., thus: CALL ONE (50). The second group includes more complicated patterns found in Movements 51–85, and are marked, e.g., thus: CALL ONE (85).

Calls that Include Selections from only the First 50 Mainstream Movements

CALL ONE (50)

All four ladies chain (four ladies chain)
(Turn the girl) you gotta chain on back
Chain back (and turn this Sue)
Join hands, circle to the left
Around you go, circle to the left
Now reverse trail, single file
Lady in the lead, gents turn around
Do an allemande left with your corner
Give a right to partner, pull on by
Grand ol' right and left
All eight step to the middle
And come on back
Four gents star by the left (a left-hand star)
One time around 'til you get back home
Do sa do around your own
Four girls star by the left (a left-hand star)
One time around, you swing and whirl
Swing around with your own girl
Left allemande with the corner. . . .

CALL TWO (50)

All four ladies chain across (four ladies chain)
First and third (second and fourth) lead out
     to the right and circle up four
Head (side) men break, you line up four
Go forward four and come on back
Right and left through right straight across
Two ladies chain straight across (turn this
     Sue)
Pass through, bend the line
Eight to the middle and come on back
Do a right and left through,
Two ladies chain straight across
(Turn this girl) pass through
Bend the line, move up to the middle and back
     right out
Do a right and left through (turn this girl)
Cross trail through to the corner one
Left allemande. . . .

CALL THREE (50)

Four ladies chain straight across
Four ladies chain back three quarters
Heads forward and back with you
Square through four hands you do
Meet the sides, right and left through
Star through, pass through, bend the line
All forward and back, right and left through
    straight across
Eight go forward and come on back, star
    through,
Right and left through
Girls rollaway with a half sashay
Box the gnat straight across, then pull her by
Allemande left. . . .

CALL FOUR (50)

Heads (sides) forward and back
Pass through, separate,
Around one to a line
Forward and back
Center four rollaway with a half sashay
All four couples rollaway
Forward eight and back
Star through, California twirl
Right and left through
Dive through, star through
Cross trail, left allemande. . . .

CALL FIVE (50)

Four ladies chain across
Four ladies chain three-quarters
Heads forward and back
Square through four hands
Right and left through with sides
Star through, pass through, bend the line
Forward and back
Right and left straight across
Forward and back
Star through right and left through
Rollaway in a half sashay
Box the gnat straight across
Pull her by, left allemande. . . .

CALL SIX (50)

First and third (second and fourth) move up
    and back
Do a right and left through (turn around with
    Jack)
Star through, then pass through
Do a right and left through and turn on
    around
Dive through, and star through in the middle
Then cross trail to the corner one
Left allemande, partner right in the right and
    left grand . . .
Heads (sides) lead to the right and circle four
Head (side) gent break to a line of four
Go forward now and back right out
Do a right and left through (turn 'em around)
Two ladies chain across the world (turn this
    around)
Pass through, California twirl
Two ladies chain across the world (turn this
    girl)
Pass through, California twirl
Eight to the middle, come on back
Star through, pass through
Do an allemande left with your left hand. . . .

CALL SEVEN (50)

Head couples up and back
Pass through across the track
Separate go around two (just two)
Get on home swing your own
Just swing and whirl
Two and four move up to the middle and
    come on back
Pass through across the track
Separate go around two (go all the way
    around)
Get on home swing the partner (swing your
    own)
Face the corner, do an allemande left. . . .

CALL EIGHT (50)

First and third go forward and back
Star through, pass through
Right and left through the outside two
Square through four hands (count to four)
Step forward, bend the line
Eight move forward and come on back
Star through, insides arch, dive through
In the middle do a right and left through
Turn this girl with a full turn around
Do a right and left through with the outside
　two
Dive through, pass through, star through with
　the outside two
Do a right and left through (and turn this girl)
Square through three quarters around
Step forward, bend the line
Move eight to the middle and back in time
Now star through, and the inside arch, and
　dive through
Pass through, do a right and left through with
　the outside two
Dive through, square through three quarters
　round to the corner one, left alle-
　mande. . . .

CALL NINE (50)

Sides (heads) move up to the middle and
　come on back
Do a right and left through (turn this girl)
Cross trail through go up the outside
Go around two, stop on the end of the line
Forward four and back you're doing fine
Two girls together do a half sashay
Two boys together do a half sashay
The couple in the middle do a half sashay
Everybody do a half sashay
Left allemande with your corner girl. . . .

CALL TEN (50)

One and three (two and four) forward and
　back with you
Now star through, and pass through
Do a right and left through with the outside
　two
(Turn this girl) and square through
Count to four (be sure it's four hands around)

Step forward, bend the line
Move eight to the middle and come on back
Now star through, insides arch, and dive
　through
In the middle do a right and left through
Turn your girl with a full turn around
Right and left through with the outside two
Dive through, pass through
Star through with the outside two
Right and left through
Square through three quarters
Step forward, bend the line
Eight to the middle and come on back in time
Star through, insides arch, outsides dive
　through
Pass through, right and left through with the
　outside two
Dive through, square through three quarters
　round
To the corner one, left all allemande. . . .

CALL ELEVEN (50)

Four ladies chain go across the floor
Heads (sides) lead to the right, circle up four
Head (side) men break make a line
Forward and back you're doing fine
Pass through, ends trade, centers run
Bend the line, go forward and back
Pass through, ends trade, centers run
Bend the line, eight to the middle and back
　with you
Star through, do an eight chain one, left
　allemande. . . .

CALL TWELVE (50)

Heads move up to the middle and come on
　back
Pass through, separate, go around one to a line
　of four
Forward four and come on back
Star through, double pass through, clover leaf
Center two right and left through (turn that
　girl)
Substitute, and center two go right and left
　through
Substitute, and center two star through
Right and left through (and turn this Sue)
Slide through, square through three quarters

Left allemande . . .
Sides forward and back with you
Star through, right and left through
Pass through, swing through
Girls circulate, boys trade
Boys run, bend the line
Forward eight and come on back
Pass through, wheel and deal
Centers right and left through (turn this girl)
Pass through, swing through
Girls circulate twice, boys trade
Boys circulate once, boys run
Bend the line, forward eight and back
Right and left through (turn this Sue)
Pass through, bend the line
Forward and back you're doing fine
Star through, swing through
Girls circulate, boys trade
Boys run, bend the line
Forward and back keep in time
Right and left through (and turn the girls)
Pass through, do a wheel and deal
A double pass through, clover leaf
Center two right and left through (yes turn this girl)
Pass through, star through
Pass through, wheel and deal
Double pass through, clover leaf
Centers right and left through (turn this girl)
Pass through, swing through
Boys run go around one, bend that line
Up to the middle and back in time
Cross trail through, find the corner
Left allemande. . . .

CALL THIRTEEN (50)

Heads move into the middle and come on back
Turn through, separate, go around just one
Down the middle, do a turn through
Do a left turn through with the sides
Come in again there, heads turn through again
Centers squeeze right in
Cast off three quarters, forward eight and back
Star through, centers square through three quarters
Ends trade, left allemande, right and left grand . . .
Sides move up to the middle and back
Square through four hands, four hands around
When you get there now

Do an eight chain through, keep on going
Meet the gal with the petticoat showing
And the gal with a hole in her stocking
Shoe string flying, petticoat flopping
Same two do a right and left through (turn this Sue)
Dive through, in the middle star through
Cross trail through, left allemande. . . .

CALL FOURTEEN (50)

Four ladies chain straight across
Heads lead to the right and circle up four
Head men you break to a line
Go forward four and back you reel
Pass through, and do a wheel and deal
A double pass through, centers in
Cast off three quarters, step up to the middle and back
Pass through, and the ends trade
Same ends run around one
Squeeze right in, and cast off three quarters
Go forward and come on back
Pass through, do a wheel and deal
Double pass through, and centers in
Cast off three quarters,
Go forward now and step on back
Pass through, and the ends trade
The same ends run around one
Squeeze right in, cast off three quarters
Go forward and get on back,
Right and left through (turn this Sue)
Star through do an eight chain five, five now man alive
Say hello corner, left allemande . . .
Heads (sides) forward and back, do a half square through
Split the sides, make a line of four
Forward eight and come on back
Ends box the gnat, centers star through
Everybody pass through, do a left allemande. . . .

Calls that Include Selections from all
85 Mainstream Movements

CALL ONE (85)

One and three (two and four) go up and back
  right out
Swing through, star through, now circle up
  four with the outside two
Break right out and make a line
Eight to the middle and back
Pass through, and girls fold, curlique
Girls trade, boys run go 'round the girl
Boys trade, boys fold in front of that girl
Right and left through (and turn this Sue),
  curlique
Boys run (go 'round this Sue), and partner
  trade
Eight to the middle and come right back
Pass through, bend the line, pass through, and
  the girls fold
Do a curlique, girls trade
Swing through, girls fold, peel off
Tag your line to the right, girls fold, curlique
Scoot back, boys turn through
Boys run right go 'round that girl
Eight to the middle and come right back
Slide through, and pass through
Left allemande. . . .

CALL TWO (85)

Heads (sides) into the middle and back right
  out
Square through four hands (count 'em, four
  hands), curlique
Walk and dodge, boys fold, curlique
Boys trade, spin chain through
Boys circulate two times fellers (two times)
When you get there now boys run, boys trade
Boys fold in front of that girl, curlique

Scoot back (boys turn through), boys run
  right (around one)
Eight to the middle and come on back
Pass through, do a wheel and deal
Centers right and left through (turn that girl)
Pass through, curlique, walk and dodge
Boys fold, do a curlique
Boys trade, swing through
Boys run (go around that girl)
Couples circulate straight ahead
Wheel and deal face this two
Star through, pass through, bend that line
Up to the middle come on back
Star through, veer to the left
Wheel and deal, pass through, trade by
Star through, right and left through (and turn
  this girl)
Slide through, pass through
Left allemande. . . .

CALL THREE (85)

Head (side) two gents take your corner girl
Go up to the middle and back right out
Box the gnat straight across
Right and left through (turn this Sue)
All join hands circle to the left
Four boys move into the middle and back
Square through four, four hands around in the
  middle of the floor
Curlique with the girls
Boys run (go around one), and promenade
Don't stop, keep on movin' that gal around
Sides wheel around, right and left through
  (and turn this Sue)
Slide through, swing through, and girls circu-
  late
Boys trade, do a turn through, left allemande
Allemande left as pretty as you can. . . . .

CALL FOUR (85)

Head (side) gents take your corner girl
Go up the middle and back right out
Box the gnat, do a right and left through
All join hands circle around circle left
Four girls to the middle and back right out
To the middle, and swing through and when you get through
Spin the top, pass through, do a do sa do with the boys
(All the way around), then spin chain through
Outsides circulate two times (outsides two times)
When you get there now girls trade, boys trade
Centers trade, boys run
Everybody do a right and left through straight across, turn 'em
Star through, swing through, and when you get through
Do a turn through and find the corner, left allemande
Head ladies chain, sides rollaway with a half sashay
Heads half square through, do sa do that outside two
Make an ocean wave, you gotta rock it there
Girls trade, boys trade, centers trade
Boys run, everybody do a right and left through (turn this girl)
Now pass through, tag the line, everybody face out
Boys run, centers trade, girls trade, boys trade
Centers trade, boys run, everybody partner trade
Forward up and come right back
Star through, California twirl,
Left allemande, right and left grand. . . .

CALL FIVE (85)

Four ladies chain straight across
Heads lead out to the right, circle up four
Head men break to a line
Forward four and back right out
Right and left through, ladies lead to a Dixie chain
Go on to the next, two ladies chain
Ladies lead to a Dixie chain, on to the next two ladies chain
Ladies lead to a Dixie chain, girls go left gents go right
Find the corner, left allemande
Here we go right and left grand . . .
Heads (sides) move to the middle and come on back
Square through about four (four hands around)
Do sa do with the outside two
Star through, pass through, boys run
Scoot back, boys fold, girls turn through
Courtesy turn the pretty little Sue
Move into the middle and come right back
Pass through, bend that line
Slide through, then a right and left through
Turn that girl, star through, pass through
Boys run, scoot back, boys fold behind the girls,
Two girls turn through
Courtesy turn the pretty little girls
Move into the middle and come on back
Slide through, and left allemande. . . .

CALL SIX (85)

Four ladies chain straight across
Heads square through four hands, four hands around
Do sa do the outside two, make a wave, and balance there
All eight circulate
Swing through, boys run go around the girl
Tag the line everybody face in,
Go up to the middle and back, everybody pass through
Wheel and deal, outsides squeeze in, go forward and back
Then right and left through, turn this Sue
Star through, dive through, square through three quarters around
Left allemande, then right and left grand. . . .

CALL SEVEN (85)

Heads (sides) move up to the middle and back
Pass through, separate, go around just one and line up four,
Move into the middle and back
Pass through, ends cross fold, star through
Square through three quarters (three hands around)
Step forward now, you wanta bend that line
Eight to the middle and back
Pass through, girls cross fold, star through
Substitute, bend the line
Into the middle and back you go
Pass through, and wheel and deal, center two square through three quarters
Left allemande, right and left grand . . .
Heads into the middle, and come right back
Do a half square through, then a right and left through
Flutterwheel, when you get there now
Swing through, boys run, tag the line to the right
Girls fold, and right and left through
Dive through, pass through, do sa do the outside two
Swing through, when you get through
Box the gnat, and right and left through
Turn this girl, do sa do (go all the way around)
Make a wave, and you balance there
The girls cross fold, do an allemande left. . . .

CALL EIGHT (85)

Sides up to the middle and back
Square through the sides about four hands
Do a single circle (join both hands, circle half around)
Boys step to a wave, boys trade, boys run (go around one)
Wheel and deal and face this two, do a right and left through
Rollaway with a half sashay, single circle to a wave
Girls in the middle, girls trade, boys run
Boys fold in front of that girl, curlique,
Scoot back now, boys turn through, boys run (around one)

Into the middle and back once more
Then right and left through (turn 'em there)
Flutterwheel, sweep a quarter
Swing through, girls cross fold, boys trade
Single circle to a wave, girls trade, boys run
Couples circulate straight ahead this time and bend the line
Eight to the middle and back, pass through
Wheel and deal, and centers right and left through
Turn this girl, substitute, center two swing through
When you get through, turn through, split your outside two
Walk around one to a line of four
Forward up and back, box the gnat
Do a right and left through the other way back
Pass through, and tag the line
Everybody face in, and you go forward and back
Star through, do a "crazy" substitute (back under and back over)
Swing through now, boys circulate, boys run 'round one
Wheel and deal, face this two, right and left through (turn 'em)
Pass through, trade by, then swing through
Girls cross fold, boys trade, single circle to a wave
Girls trade, boys run, boys trade, cast off around a girl
Three quarters around, up to the middle and come right back
Star through, right and left through (turn 'em)
Then pass through, then trade by
Left allemande, grand right and left grand. . . .

CALL NINE (85)

Heads (sides) lead to the right, circle up four
Break now you make two lines, forward four and come on back
Pass through, and wheel and deal
Center two right and left through (turn that girl)
Pass through, then star through
Pass through, the ends trade
Centers run, bend the line
Up to the middle come right back

Star through, clover leaf
Center two go right and left through (turn 'em)
Pass through, star through, pass through,
Bend the line, eight to the middle and back
Pass through, tag the line, everybody face in
Go up to the middle and back
Star through, California twirl, swing through
Boys run, wheel and deal, face this two and right and left through
Star through, pass through, bend the line
Move into the middle and back
Slide through, right and left through
Swing through, boys run, bend the line
Go up to the middle, get on back, star through
Do an eight chain one, left allemande, grand right and left. . . .

CALL TEN (85)

Heads (sides) move into the middle and back
Do a half square through, swing through
Girls circulate twice, boys trade
Boys circulate once, boys run
Go around the girl, and bend the line
Eight to the middle and back, then a right and left through
Rollaway with a half sashay
Forward four and come right back
Spin the top, swing through
Boys run, tag the line to the right
Girls fold, do a curlique
Scoot back, turn through boys
Boys fold, two ladies chain straight across turn this Jane
Move into the middle and come on back
Pass through, wheel and deal
Center two right and left through (turn this girl)
Pass through, star through, then a right and left through
Ladies lead to a Dixie style ocean wave, and balance there
Girls run, girls trade, cast off around the boys,
Move into the middle and come right back, slide through
Chain through, girls circulate two times (two times ladies)
When you get there, boys run, now tag the line
Face to the right, do a wheel and deal and face this two

Swing through and the boys cross fold
Girls trade, single circle to a wave
Boys trade, girls run, girls fold in front of that boy
Curlique, scoot back, girls turn through, walk and dodge
(Boys walk) boys fold in front of that girl, curlique
Boys trade, swing through, boys run, and boys trade
Couples circulate straight ahead
Bend the line, up to the middle and back
Right and left through, pass through
Wheel and deal, square through, five hands (five, four, three, two, one)
Left allemande, weave the ring. . . .

CALL ELEVEN (85)

First and third (second and fourth) up to the middle come on back
Do a half square through, swing through, girls fold
Peel off, wheel and deal face this two
Star through, pass through, tag that line, everybody face out
Boys run, centers trade, girls trade, boys trade, centers trade
Boys run, do a partner trade, and a quarter more (look at her)
Single circle halfway, girls trade
Girls run, tag the line to the right, wheel and deal
Face this two, right and left through, turn this girl
Dive through, substitute, centers right and left through with a full turn around,
Left allemande, right and left grand. . . .

CALL TWELVE (85)

Heads (sides) flutterwheel across the town
Then square through two hands around
Swing through, to a curlique
Split circulate, then walk and dodge
Bend the line, **left allemande** . . .
Heads square through four hands around
Curlique, and hinge, centers trade
Hinge once more, boys run, curlique
Cast off three quarters, centers trade
Pass through, left allemande. . . .

CALL THIRTEEN (85)

Heads (sides) to the right, circle to a line
Forward and back you're doing fine
Everybody whirlaway with a half sashay
Turn and left through (turn 'em boys)
Swing through, turn and left through
Spin the top and when you're through
Turn and left through, star through
Right and left through (turn the girls around)
Cross trail to a left allemande . . .
Heads (sides) star through, right and left
    through
Pass through, swing through, boys trade
Turn and left through, dive through, pass
    through
Swing through, boys trade, turn and left
    through

Pass to the center, right and left through
    (turn the girls)
Square through three quarters, allemande
    left. . . .

CALL FOURTEEN (85)

Heads (sides) square through four hands
    around
(Count 'em now go four around the town)
Do sa do with those you face
Circle left make a line in place
Forward four and back with you
Do sa do, make an ocean wave
Recycle now and two face two
Right and left through like you always do
Flutterwheel go across the town
Cross trail through and left allemande. . . .

Calls for Openings and Breaks

Allemande left your corner maid
Swing your partner and promenade. . . .

All eight to the middle and come on back
Allemande left your corner, give a right to
    partner
Right and left grand. . . .

Heads forward and back right there
Sides face and Grand Square
Walk two, three, turn, walk two, three, turn
Walk two, three, turn, walk two, three, reverse
Walk two, three, turn, walk two, three, turn
Walk two, three, turn, walk two, left allemande
Allemande left with your left hand
Right to partner in a right and left grand. . . .

Join eight hands circle left that way
Ladies to the center, gents left sashay
Once more, ladies to the center, gents left
    sashay
Circle left, whirlaway with a half sashay
Swing that girl coming your way
And promenade. . . .

Bow to partner, and corners too
Join hands and circle to the left you do
Circle left around you go
Do an allemande left with corner
Pull partner by for a right and left grand. . . .

Heads (sides) move up to the middle and
    come on back
Do sa do walk around that opposite girl one
    time
Make a right-hand star
Star by the right go one time around to the
    corner
Allemande left with your corner girl. . . .

Bow to partners and corners all
Join hands and circle the hall
Break and trail home along the line
Swing at home you're doing fine.

Join hands circle left, allemande left
Curlique your own to an Alamo style
Rock it up and back (balance)
Boys run, allemande left. . . .

Gents right-hand star in the center of the town
Once around with the right foot up, left
    foot down
Allemande left with your corner maid
Back to partner and promenade. . . .

Allemande left then weave the ring
Weave in and out around you go
When you meet your own do sa do
Then promenade go two-by-two
Get along home like you always do. . . .

All to the center with a left-hand star
Turn it now but not too far
Back with the right go around the track
Girls turn back on the outside track
Left-hand swing with your own man
Roll promenade around the land. . . .

Allemande left with corners all
Then grand sashay around the hall
Do sa do your own, pull by right hand
Sashay the next, pull by left hand
Do sa do the next, right-hand pull-by
Sashay the next, left-hand pull-by
Swing your own and promenade. . . .

Head (side) couples star through, zoom
    around two
Centers right and left through, zoom around
    two
Centers pass through, left allemande. . . .

Heads pair off, corners do sa do
Then allemande left around you go
Swing partners right, but not too far
Change hands to a left for an allemande thar
Men back in make a backward star
Roll promenade like a Cadillac car. . . .

Bow to partners and corners all
Circle eight go 'round that hall
Face partners now do a do paso
Swing partner by the left, corner by the right
Partner left like an allemande thar
Slip the clutch, left allemande
Here we go, right and left grand. . . .

Bow to your partner and your corner girl
Left allemande to an allemande thar
Right and left and the four gents star
Gents star right but not too far
Shoot that star make it whirl
Go right and left to a brand-new girl
Gents back in to a brand-new star
Back right up where you are
Shoot that star and meet your own
Promenade that pretty girl home. . . .

All eight to the middle and back you go
Left allemande, don't be slow
Right and left grand. . . .

Bow to your partner, give her a swing
Circle to the left around the ring
Do an allemande left with your left hand
Here we go, right and left grand. . . .

Bow to partners and corners all
Circle eight around that hall
Circle left around you go
Break the ring with a do paso
Partner by the left, corner by the right
Partner left like an allemande thar
Gents back up in a backward star
Slip the clutch, left allemande
Here we go in a right and left grand. . . .

All around your left-hand lady
Left-hand turn your pretty little taw
Four ladies chain straight across
Chain 'em back, don't get lost

Walk all around your corner lady
Seesaw around your pretty taw
Allemande left, allemande thar
Go right and left, four gents star
Left-arm swing make a backward star
Shoot the star go all the way around
Give a right to the corner make a wrong way
    thar
Men back in to a left-hand star
Everybody do a U turn back
Slip the clutch to a left allemande
Partner right in a right and left grand. . . .

Heads (sides) move up to the middle and back
Do sa do, make a right-hand star
Left allemande
Right and left grand
Promenade, don't slow down
Put the girls in front go single file
Girls turn around and swing awhile
Face the corner, do an allemande left
Right and left grand . . .

Allemande left your corner girl
Promenade partner around the world
And go red hot
Turn the right-hand lady with a right turn
    through
Partner with a left all around you do
To your corner lady with a left hand around
Promenade partner around the town.

Left-hand swing your corners around
Right and left grand around the town
Oats in the barn, wheat in the stack
When you meet your own you turn right back
Left and right grand go the wrong way
Turn back again when you meet your Kay
Right and left grand. . . .

Ladies chain across to the opposite man
All chain back, go home again
Roll promenade go around the town
With the right foot up and the left foot
    down. . . .

Heads (sides) forward and back
Pass through, separate, go around two
Swing your own
Face the corner, do an allemande left
Allemande left as pretty as you can
Right to partner right and left grand
Right and left around you go
Meet your own and do sa do
Do sa do then promenade. . . .

Join eight hands and circle the town
Circle now to the left around
Circle to the left don't be slow
Break the circle with a do paso
Partner left, left hand around
Corner with the right around the town
Partner left, left all around
Back to corner and catch all eight
Right hand halfway around
Back with the left, left hand around
Swing your partner, promenade the town.

Calls for Endings

Bow to corners and partners all
Wave at the pretty girl across the hall
That's it, that's all.

Allemande left with your left hand
Bow to your own and there you stand.

All eight to the middle and back right out
Bow to partners and corners too
Hold her there, that's it, you're through.

Promenade, you know where and I don't care
Take her out to a rocking chair.

You swing her, and she swings you, and
    promenade
A little piece of corn bread layin' on the shelf
If you want any more just call it yourself.

Promenade, you know where and I don't care
Take her out and give her some air.

Fill-in Patter for Grand Right and Left, Weave the Ring

Promenade that's what I said
If she don't like biscuits, feed her corn bread.

Ingo, bingo six penny high
A big pig, a little pig, root hog or die.

Honey in a gourd and a gourd on the ground
When you meet your honey gonna promenade
    around.

Meet old Sal, meet old Kate
Meet your own promenade eight.

Meet that gal with a hole in her stocking
Shoe string flying, petticoat flopping.

Promenade go high and wide
Promenade on all four sides.

Hand over hand and heel over heel
The more you dance the better you feel.

Do the right and left grand
Meet every other one with every other hand.

Hurry up cowboy don't be slow
You won't go to heaven if you don't do so.

Selected Singing Calls

ALABAMA JUBILEE

This dance, arranged by Joe Lewis, was the first singing square dance call done in ragtime rhythm. The form is slightly different from later standard arrangements. Original version. INTRO RECORDS, 7000 Series, No. 50

Figure (four times):

It's the Alabama Jubliee . . .
Four little ladies promenade inside the ring
Go back and swing that guy, swing and swing
Sashay that corner girl one time around
You're gonna bow to your partner now, then
    swing that guy go 'round and 'round
Four men promenade inside the hall
Go back and sashay (do sa do), go round
    'em all

That corner girl give her a swing
Take her around the ring
To that Alabama Jubilee.

Ending:

Come on it's all join hands, circle left
    make that big old ring
Break the ring with the corner swing
    leave her on the right you're gone again
Ring, ring, that pretty little ring
It's break it again with a corner swing
Leave her on the right you're gone again
Circle left and don't you know
Do si do (today's do paso) and a little more
    dough take the girl and home you go
Stop when you get home, there's time you
    know

All around that old left-hand lady, seesaw
  around that taw
Then swing that opposite girl across the hall
Promenade her home you all
You've got your partner, you've got your maid
Take that gal and promenade
All around your left-hand lady, seesaw your
  taw
It's allemande left with that old left hand
Partner right in a right and left grand
Here's Sal, here's Sue, here's the gal that
  came with you
Take 'em home get on that old choo-choo
Promenade around that ring, get 'em happy
  boys
Give 'em a swing . . . it's the Alabama Jubilee.

ALABAMA JUBILEE
(Singing Square Dance—Later Version)

Caller: Bruce Johnson
Dance composer: Joe Lewis
Record: Windsor, No. 4144/4444

**Sequence: Opener, Figure (twice),
Middle Break, Figure (twice), closer**

Opener:

Well, bow to your partner, the gal by your side
All join hands and circle left, you circle out
  wide
Walk all around that left-hand lady, seesaw
  'round your taw
Back to the corner with your left hand,
  allemande left—go right and left grand
Right foot high, the left foot low, meet your
  honey and you do sa do
Do sa do on the heel and toe, then step right
  up and swing her, Joe
You swing her once, and swing her again, then
  promenade the ring
To the Alabama Jubilee, whoo-ee (tag) to the
  Alabama Jubilee

Figure:

Four little ladies promenade, go 'round the in-
  side ring
Come back home and swing your man, you
  swing and you swing
Walk all around that left-hand lady, bow down
  to your own
Now swing your honey, go round and round,
  any ol' way but upside down
Four men promenade, you go round the inside
  ring
Come back home and do sa do, then corners
  you'll swing
Swing that corner 'round and 'round, then you
  promenade to town
To the Alabama Jubilee, oh, me (tag) to the
  Alabama Jubilee

Four ladies promenade ccw around inside of
set back to partners, partners swing, walk all
around corners, bow to partners, swing partners. Four gents promenade ccw around inside
of set back to partners, partners do sa do,
corners swing and promenade full around set
back to gents' home positions, ending with all
having original corners for new partners.

Middle Break and Closer:

Well, turn the left-hand lady with the left-hand
  round, back to your honey with a right-
  hand round
Twice around your partners go, to the right-
  hand lady with a left elbow
Back to your honey and swing her, men, swing
  her quick, we're gone again
Allemande left with your left hand, here we go
  —right and left grand
Big foot high, little foot low, meet your gal and
  you do sa do
One time around on the heel and toe, then step
  right up and swing her, Joe
You swing her once, and swing her again, then
  promenade the ring
To the Alabama Jubilee, whoo-ee (tag) to the
  Alabama Jubilee

JUST BECAUSE
(Singing Square Dance—Earlier Version)

Caller: Bruce Johnson
Record: Windsor, No. 4444/4144

Sequence: Opener, Figure (twice for Head Ladies), Middle Break, Figure (twice for Side Ladies), Closer

Opener, Middle Break and Closer:

Walk all around your corner, she's the gal
    from Arkansaw
Seesaw 'round your partners, gents star right
    around that hall
And when you meet your corners, do a left
    allemande
Now walk around that circle with a right and
    left grand
When you meet your honey, do a do sa do
Step right up and swing her high and low
Then promenade that ring, throw your heads
    right back and sing
(all sing) "Because just because . . ."

Figure:

Well, the two head ladies chain right on over
Same two ladies chain back again
Side two ladies chain right on over
Same two ladies chain back again
Allemande left your corners, allemande right
    your partners
Go back and swing that sweet corner gal
Then promenade that corner, boys, shout and
    sing with joy
(all sing) "Because, just because . . ."
Tag (all sing)
"Because, just because . . ."

JUST BECAUSE
(Singing Square Dance Call—Later Version)

Caller: Bailey Campbell
Record: Kalox No. K-1157

Sequence: Opener, Figure (twice for heads), Middle Break, Figure (twice for sides)

Opener and Middle Break:

Four ladies promenade, go walking 'round the
    ring
Home you go swing the handsome man
Allemande ole corner turn partner by the right
Four men promenade go 'round the ring to-
    night
Home you go and do sa do
Left allemande and promenade and go
I'm telling you, baby, I'm thru with you
Because, just because . . .

Figure:

Head (side) couples promenade go halfway
    'round
Two and four (one and three) do the right
    and left thru
The sides (heads) curlique, the boys run right
Do sa do once around, eight chain four tonight
Count four hands across, swing number five
Swing that girl and promenade, oh, man alive
I'm telling you, baby, I'm thru with you
You've done your daddy wrong.

OH, JOHNNY, OH
(Singing Square Dance Call)

Callers: Don and Marie Armstrong
Record: Lloyd Shaw Recordings, Inc.,
    No. 3301

CALL

All join hands and you circle the ring
Stop where you are, give your partner a swing
Then swing that corner girl
Go back and swing your own, swing and whirl

Allemande left with the girl on your left
Do sa do your own
Take your corner and promenade, go walking
    with your maid
Singing Oh, Johnny, Oh.

SUMMER SOUNDS
(Singing Square Dance Call)

Records: MacGregor—2051-A
          Blue Star—BS-1021-B

Introduction, Break, Ending:

Circle left . . .
Listen to the music of the carousel
The ting-alinga-lingle of the ice cream bell

or,

The paddle of a steamer on a Sunday cruise
The sizzle of a hot dog at a barbecue

or,

Shrieking of a roller coaster away up high
The whistles on the beach as a peach walks by

Allemande left your corner, your partners do
    sa do
Gents star left once around you go
(All promenade)

Do sa do the partner, with the corners
    allemande
Come back and promenade the land

Here come summer sounds, the summer
    sounds I love.

Figure:

Heads (Sides) . . .
Star through, pass through, circle round the
    track
(Four Ladies promenade, go once inside the
    ring)

Head men break and make a line, go forward
    up and back
(Gents swing your partner, yes, swing that
    pretty Jane)

Pass through, wheel and deal, centers star
    through
(Allemande left your corner, do sa do your
    own)

Pass through, clover leaf, the new center two
(Four Gents promenade one time around you
    roam)

Square through, three quarters, turn corner by
    the left
(You do sa do the partner, and your own lady
    swing)

All the way around, promenade this pet
(Swing your girl and promenade that ring)

Here come summer sounds, the summer
    sounds I love.

The Special Language of Square Dancing:
A Selected Glossary

Square dancing has a special language all its own. Some of the words are simple directional terms, and others are coined folk expressions developed through the years. Square dancers and callers must understand the language in order to take part in the activity.

Much of this language is explained in the sections giving eighty-five *Mainstream Movements* of modern square dancing and fifteen *Oldies but Goodies*. Here is a selected listing and explanation of other pertinent terminology.

Across the Set From home position, the opposite place across the square. In facing lines, from one line to the other.

Active Dancer(s) Those designated in the call to perform the movement.

Arky Couple A couple made up of either two men or two women.

Balance Designated dancers step forward with one foot and touch the toe of the free foot beside it, then step backward with the free foot and touch the toe of the other foot beside it.

Behind You The person directly in back of the active dancer.

Break Release hands.

Break and Trail Release hands (while circling) and go single file.

Caller The person who chants or sings or says the "calls" that direct square dancers through the movements of square dancing.

Calls—Singing, Patter (see Part V *Calling, Teaching, Calls*, etc.) A *Singing Call* incorporates specific "calls" set to a particular tune like a song. Some of the song lyrics are replaced by "calls" for square dance movements; other lyrics are included to allow time for completion of the movements.

A *Patter* or *"Hash" Call* is flexible and does not necessarily rhyme. It is made up of smooth-flowing combinations of "calls" directing movements freely chosen by the caller and called in time to any tune selected. Each patter call usually emphasizes different ways of doing two or three selected movements. No two patter calls are exactly alike.

"Calls" Commands or directions using familiar wording combined with special coined terminology to direct designated (active) dancers through specific movements. "Calls" are segments of a complete square dance call. Some "calls" denote combinations of several simpler movements; these must be learned by the dancers. The "calls" are chanted, sung, or said by the caller in rhythm to music. A "call" must be timed to precede the action slightly while the previous movement is being done so the dancers will know in advance what to do next. Some "calls" are directed to the gents, with the lady automatically performing a counterpart movement; others are to a couple (active) while another couple automatically does the counterpart.

Centers Those in the inside area of the square, or the center of a formation such as a line.

Challenge Dancing Complicated movements danced by those with expertise beyond that of the average dancer.

Counterpart Action Automatic action other than that designated in the "call."

Couple—Standard, Arky, Mixed Two dancers standing side-by-side facing the same direction make up a couple. In a *standard* couple the gent has a lady at his right; an *arky* couple is made up of either two ladies or two gents; a *mixed* couple has the gent at the lady's right side.

Cue(s) Word or words giving directions for dancers' actions.

Designations Names and positions of the dancers in relation to the square formation and other dancers.

Divide Designated dancers move sideways away from each other.

Don't Stop, Don't Slow Down A call directing dancers who are promenading, not to stop or slow down at home position.

Duple Time The combining of rhythmic pulses into successive groups having like arrangement and duration (2/4, 4/4, 6/8 time).

Elbow Hook One dancer hooks an elbow with another.

Ends Those in the outside position of a line or formation.

Face—Those Two, to the Middle, In, Out, Your Own, the Sides, etc. Active dancer(s) turn to face the direction or person indicated.

Figure A series of movements making up a dance pattern.

Hoedown Traditional fiddle band square dance music or tune.

Inactive Dancer(s) Dancers who remain in place, ready to take part in a movement that includes them, or to do a counterpart movement.

Indian Style Single file.

Inside The area in front of the dancers when in home positions. Inside also refers to those nearest the middle of a line or formation.

Inside Hands Adjacent hands of people standing side-by-side.

Lead Dancer(s) or Couple Those who are followed by other dancers or are the first to initiate an action.

Line Dancers standing in a line shoulder-to-shoulder. A "two-faced" line has two dancers at each end of the line facing opposite directions.

Look Her in the Eye Face partner.

Mainstream Dancing Movements most widely being danced consistently.

Make an Arch Two dancers raise joined hands forming an arch with their arms.

Maneuver Slight movement sideways that adjusts the position(s) of the dancer(s) to complete the action properly.

Movement An action or combination of actions performed by designated (active) dancers while those in the set not designated (inactive) do the counterpart or stand in place until a movement including them is called. Each movement is directed by a square dance "call."

Music for Square Dancing May be almost any tune, hoedown, or popular tune, with a strong, steady rhythm, in duple time, between 128 and 134 metronome beats per minute. It can be played on a record player, tape recorder, or by live musicians on almost any instrument.

New—Lines of Four, Partners, etc. For "new lines of four," from two parallel lines of four (two couples each), dancers follow a movement ending with each of the couples paired with a new couple in a new line perpendicular to the original lines. For "new partners," dancers making up a couple are separated during a movement, and each ends up in position with another dancer as partner.

Outside An area behind the dancers when in home positions. Outside also refers to those farthest away from the center of a star promenade formation, to those on the outside ends of a line formation, and dancers outside of others who are inside.

Outside Hands Hands on opposite or far sides of a couple or line of dancers standing side-by-side.

Pack Saddle Star This is formed by designated dancers extending the same (left or right) hand toward each other and lightly grasping the wrist of the person ahead.

Party Square Dancing Easy dances for one-night stands or groups that only dance occasionally at parties or recreational programs.

Pigeon Wing Hand clasp with elbows bent upward.

Plateaus or Skill Levels The plateau or skill level is determined by the number of mainstream movements that the caller and dancers have mastered, but there are no clear delineations between levels of dancing.

Program Enough tips spaced with rest periods and round dances or mixers to last between two and three hours.

Pull-by A part of many movements wherein two facing dancers briefly join right (or left) hands and pass right shoulders (or left shoulders) as they gently pull by each other, release hands, and end back-to-back.

Rock It Same as balance.

Roll Back Designated dancer or couple turns away from the dancer or couple beside him or her to reverse the direction faced.

Set The same as a "square."

Skirt Work Ladies flare skirts at the sides by holding them out from the body.

Spread It Wide Dancers with arms around each other's waists move apart sideways to handclasp position with arms outstretched.

Step for Modern Square Dancing A light, gliding walk without skips or jerks.

Step Through Dancers facing alternate directions in a line release hands and step forward out of the line.

Straight Ahead Move forward without turning around.

Square Four couples (male-female) of dancers standing with one couple facing in from each side of an imaginary square.

Square Dancer One of eight people making up a square dance "set" or "square."

Styling This is *how* the movements are performed—smoothness, gracefulness, flourishes such as twirls, holding skirt out, hands in proper position, etc.

Swing the One Behind You Active dancer turns to face and swing a dancer following him or her.

Those Who Can Dancers in position to perform the particular movement called.

Tip A segment of a square dance program, usually made up of either two or three calls, including both "patter" and "singing" calls. A tip is followed by a rest period and often a round dance.

Trailing Dancer(s) or Couple Those who are facing in the same direction as, and following, other dancers.

Wrong Way Opposite from the normal or accepted direction.

The standard symbol for square dancing and round dancing.

III

FIFTEEN OLDIES BUT GOODIES
WITH CALLS

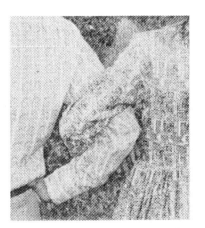

Elbow hook in a star promenade.

Lest They Be Lost

Through the years, modern square dance developments have altered or pushed aside many delightful traditional figures and movements. In an effort to reclaim a few of these, fifteen old-timers are given here—some from pioneer days, others from later times. Some are adapted in order to fit them into the modern-day format of terminology and structure.

These dances may be danced purely for pleasure or presented as demonstrations or exhibitions on historical or other types of programs. Learning them provides an excellent link between modern times and the activities of yesteryear. Those with simple choreography are easily performed and especially enjoyed by children as well as grown-ups.

Square dance steps in early days included spirited two-steps, such as the Abilene two-step "lift," jig steps, and even the tap dance clog-steps as demonstrated in the square dancing done on Grand Ole Opry TV programs. Using one of these steps when dancing the old-time figures and movements is fun and adds variety. Directions for the steps are given in the round dance section of this book.

TEXAS STAR
An old figure dance

From home positions, ladies dance forward and back (or with inside hands joined, each gent leads his partner around to face him, then she makes a left-face turn under his arched right arm back to place), then gents make a right-hand star (eight steps), change hands and make a left-hand star, pass partners by, and pick up their right-hand ladies for a star promenade. Gents back out, ladies go in (inside out, outside in) (for a variation, turn 1½ times) reverse star promenade (eight steps). Ladies back out, gents go in to star promenade again. Gents break the star and back out to positions for all to circle left. Gents stop at home place with new partners. The pattern is danced four times until each lady is back with her partner.

CALL

Ladies to the center, back to the bar
Gents to the center make a right-hand star

Right hand across "Howdy do?"
Left hand back "How are you?"

Meet your pretty girl pass her by
Pick up the next girl on the fly (*make a Texas star*)

Gents back out, *Ladies* go in
Make that Texas star (reverse promenade) again

Ladies back out, *Gents* in once more
Make a Texas star in the middle of the floor

Gents back out and all circle eight
Circle back to place 'til you get straight.

"*Texas star . . .*"

CAGE THE BIRD: three hands, seven hands

An old figure dance

For *Cage the Bird Three Hands,* with dancers in home positions, the couple designated leads to the right and circles with that couple. The lead lady (the bird) steps inside the circle, while the other three circle around her. (The bird whirls around, holding arms out like wings, and "cheeps" like a bird.) Then the bird exchanges places with her partner (the crow) in the circle. (The crow flaps his arms like wings and "caws" like a crow.) The gent then takes his original place in the circle. When on the inside of the circle, the lead couple leaves and visits each of the other couples in consecutive order and repeats the movement.

"Cage the bird three hands around . . ."

For *Cage the Bird Seven Hands,* with dancers in home positions, the lead gent moves from one position to another to right-arm-swing his right-hand lady, left-arm-swing his left-hand lady, two-hand-swing his opposite lady, two-hand-swing his partner, then put her

(the bird) in the center while he joins the others in circling around her. (The bird whirls around and "cheeps.") The lead lady and gent (the crow) exchange places. (The crow flaps his arms like wings and "caws" loudly.) All gents two-hand-swing their partners and promenade.

CALL I

First (Second, Third, Fourth) Couple to the
  right and circle four
Cage the Bird and circle three

Bird flies out, crow hops in
Three hands up you're gone again

Crow hops out and circle four
Lead couple* on to the next and circle four.

 *Repeat the pattern with each of the other couples, then return to home place.

CALL II

Number One (Two, Three, Four) Gent lead
  to the right

Swing your right-hand lady with the right hand
  around
Then your left-hand lady with the left hand
  around

Give your opposite lady a two-hand swing
Swing your partner and put her in the ring

. . . and *Seven Hands* around

Now the bird hops out the old crow in
Seven Hands up you're gone again

Crow hops out, everybody swing
And promenade home around the ring.

FIGURE EIGHT
An old figure dance

With dancers in home positions, the lead gent joins inside hands with his lady and goes ahead leading her to the couple at their right and into a figure eight pattern in between and around the lady, then the gent. He goes ahead of his partner between that couple, passing with his back toward the inactive lady (as she moves forward temporarily to make more space), then in between the couple and faces toward the inactive gent (as he moves forward temporarily) while passing around him until in place with couples facing. The two couples join hands, circle one time around, and the lead gent breaks his left-hand grasp and pulls the three dancers in a line to go between the next couple to repeat the figure eight pattern. After six have circled, he again breaks his left-hand grasp and pulls the other five in a line to the last couple to repeat the figure eight pattern, then all eight circle back to home positions.

"Do the figure eight . . ."

 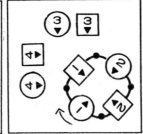

"Go around the lady, do the figure eight . . ."   *"Circle up four . . ."*

"Then pull your freight, go around the next lady . . ."

CALL

First (Second, Third, Fourth) old *couple* lead out to the right
Do the figure eight if it takes all night

Go around that lady do the figure eight
Back around the gent, don't be late
Ring up four then pull your freight

Go around the next lady and do the figure eight
Back around the gent 'til you get straight

Chase the rabbit chase the squirrel
Chase that pretty girl around the world

All join hands and circle six
Circle left like picking up sticks

Lead Gent lead to the next
Around the lady do the figure eight
Back around the gent don't be late

Chase the rabbit chase the squirrel
Chase that pretty girl around the world

Chase the rabbit, chase the (rac)'coon
Chase that big boy around the room

Join hands and circle eight
Circle back home 'til you get straight.

WAGON WHEEL (Right Hand Over, Left Hand Under)
DENVER WAGON WHEEL (Triple Duck)

An old figure dance. The "triple duck" movement is often used in exhibitions; this is a modified version.

For *Wagon Wheel,* two opposite gents stand in place alone while the other two opposite gents each stand in a line between two ladies. The lines of three join inside hands, dance forward, and the end ladies join hands; then keeping the lines straight, they circle left to exchange sides. The end ladies release hands, and each line backs up to the opposite place. The lone gents exchange places passing right shoulders. Each gent in the line now leads the ladies on either side forward until they face each other in front of him. He makes an arch with the lady at his right and leads the lady at his left under it (*Right Hand Over, Left Hand Under*), then he releases their hands so each can dance straight ahead and turn to positions (three in a line) at the sides of different lone gents.

For *Denver Wagon Wheel (Triple Duck),* two opposite gents stand in place alone while the other two opposite gents each stand three in a line between two ladies. The lines of three (with joined inside hands) dance forward, each gent releases hands with the lady at his left, gents take left forearms with each other and make arches with the ladies at their right sides. All six dance forward in circular directions (couples ccw, lone ladies cw), left-hand ladies bending their knees to duck under, as arches pass over them three times. All hands are released, and each lady turns around to stand in a line of three beside a lone gent. Left-hand ladies stop at the left side of the lone gent who was at their right, right-hand ladies at the right side of the lone gent who was at their left. The two remaining lone gents continue the left-arm turn with each other and go to opposite sides from their starting positions.

"Right hand over, left hand under . . ."

"Do a triple duck . . ."

CALL I

First (Second, Third, Fourth) Couple out to
    the couple on the right
Circle four with all your might

Leave that lady where she be
(*Gent*) on to the next and circle three

Steal that girl like honey from a bee
On to the next circle four you see

Leave that girl and go home alone.

Six to the center and back with you*
Lonesome gents go up and back too

Six to the center and *Wagon Wheel* around
Lone gents change places across the town

Right Hand Over, Left Hand Under
Hurry up girls don't you blunder.

    *Repeat three times from here.

CALL II

Heads (*Sides*) lead right, circle four around
Head (*Side*) *Gents* go back to your hometown

Forward three and back in a line*
Lone Gents up and back in time

Forward Six, Gents join left arms

Right hand high, left lady under
A Triple Duck and don't you blunder

Over and under around you go
Then line up three again you know

And . . .

    *Repeat three times from here.

SPINNING WHEEL
An old dance often used in exhibitions

From a single-file promenade, all make a left-hand star (spokes) and at the same time put tips of right fingers on the right shoulder of the person ahead (rim). To reverse the wheel, all turn back left face, make a right-hand star, and put left fingers on the left shoulder of the person ahead.

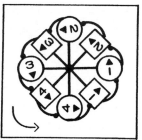

"*Spinning wheel . . .*"

"*Make a spinning wheel . . .*"

CALL

All join hands circle awhile
The other way back go Indian file

Make a *Spinning Wheel* roll it along
Now turn back, you done gone wrong

Make a new *Spinning Wheel* roll it around
With the right foot up, the left one down

Ladies turn back to a left allemande
Promenade home around the land.

TWO STARS (in the night) (VENUS AND MARS)

A modified version of an old dance

With all dancers turning in a star promenade, number one (two, three, four) lady leads out to the right to begin forming a right-hand star, and the other ladies join her in consecutive order. Both stars turn around once (or twice if preferred) until the lead lady is adjacent to her partner. Without stopping the turning stars, partners slide past each other (half sashay) to exchange places; (he sidesteps behind her to join the right-hand star, as she sidesteps in front of him to his place in the left-hand star). In quick succession the following couples switch stars until all ladies are in the left-hand star and all gents are in the right-hand star, being careful to hold the star formations while changing. When the lead couple is again adjacent, they start a change back until all are back in original stars. The next time around, the lead gent picks up his partner with an arm around, and each in turn does the same until all are in a star promenade.

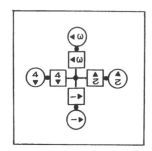

"All star promenade . . ."

*". . . head lady lead out
and make two stars . . ."*

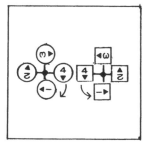

*". . . and turn those
stars . . ."*

"All star promenade . . ."

". . . head lady leads out . . ."

"... to make two stars ..."

CALL

Gents to the center make a left-hand star
Turn it around right where you are

Pick up your partner as you come around
Star promenade around the town

The *Head Lady* leads out to the right
To *Make Two* beautiful *Stars* in the night

Turn the stars go twice around
With the right foot up and the left foot down

Now change over a girl and a boy
As you come dancing around with joy

Change back a boy and a girl
As you come dancing around the world

Gents pick up your partners with an arm
        around
Star promenade around the town.

TAKE A PEEK (SWING OR CHEAT)
An old figure dance

With two standard couples facing, the active couple divides and leans forward to "peek" at each other behind the other couple (the inactive couple may twist around and look too). Then they go back to each other and swing (or the lady may "cheat" at the last minute by turning away and swinging with the inactive gent).

"Take a peek ..."

CALL

First (Second, Third, Fourth) Couple bow
        and then you swing
Lead on out to the right of the ring

Go around that couple and *Take a Peek**
Back to your own and *Swing—or Cheat*

Around that couple and peek once more
Now circle up four in the middle of the floor

Leave that couple go on to the next.†

   *Repeat from here for Couples 3 and 4.

   †Substitute "home" for "on to the next" after dancing with the last couple.

FOUR/EIGHT HANDS OVER (FLAP THE GIRLS) (MAKE A BASKET)

A modified version of an old dance often used in exhibitions

Note: In *Flap the Girls*, the ladies' feet are swung off the floor. Be sure there is plenty of space so the flying feet will not strike a wall, chair, or person.

Preliminary positioning is the same for *Flap the Girls* and *Make a Basket*. Two (for *Four Hands over*) or four (for *Eight Hands over*) standard couples face in, and the ladies join hands and make a circle inside a circle made by the gents. Each lady stands (on tiptoe for *Flap the Girls*) between her partner and the gent at his right (gents' joined hands will be behind her); gents squat slightly (keeping backs straight) while ladies raise joined hands over the heads of the two gents beside them; then gents stand up straight. All circle left.

For *Make a Basket,* ladies allow their joined hands to drop to the gents' waist level, creating a woven basket effect with arms crisscrossed behind dancers. All dancers arch their backs slightly and hold heads back to create a flaring basket effect, then sidestep to the left or right in unison.

For *Flap the Girls,* the ladies change their handgrasps to a firm hold of the men's upper shoulders, and gents change to a firm, supportive hold around each girl's lower rib cage. (Firm but not rough holds are necessary to keep the girls from slipping.) All arch their backs, hold heads back, and gradually accelerate the pace. Centrifugal force will lift the girls' feet from the floor. (Girls should hold legs and feet together and point toes.) The faster the pace, the higher the girls' feet will go. With practice the gents can raise and lower their arms to "flap the girls" up and down.

To finish either movement, gents hold on firmly to assist ladies to regain their balance, then all slide apart, join hands, and circle until sure that no one is dizzy.

"Make a basket . . ."

"Flap the girls . . ."

CALL I

Head (Side, All) Ladies circle left inside right
 there
Gents circle right outside of the square

Four (Eight) Hands over and *Gents* duck under
Make a basket circle left like thunder

Circle to the right around the town
Spread the basket, circle left around.

CALL II

Head (Side, All) Ladies circle left
Gents circle right like thunder
Four (Eight) Hands over and *Gents* bow under

Hug those girls and don't you blunder
Flap them boys, flap like thunder

Let 'em down and circle the ring
Home you go and all eight swing.

HEEL AND TOE (HAYLOFT) POLKA SQUARE

An old figure dance that incorporates a polka step into the square dance and is sometimes used in exhibitions

"Heel and toe polka square."

With dancers in home positions, designated opposite couples divide (step apart), and the remaining couples quarter out (turn back-to-back). Corners, now facing, join both hands (rights to lefts) and sashay (sidestep four steps) to the center, sashay back to place, and sashay to the center again. They release hands and move into a single line, with each lady standing directly in front of the gent who was beside her. Each lady with a gent behind her will face another lady. Ladies may hold up both hands about shoulder height for the gents to grasp, or ladies may hold skirts out at both sides while gents place their hands at the sides of the ladies' waists.

For the heel and toe polka step, each dancer should stand on the right foot, extend the left leg sideward, and touch left heel to the floor

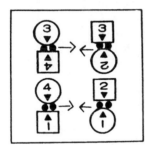

"Head couples divide . . . side couples quarter out . . ."

"Do a heel and toe . . ."

with toes pointing up, then bring the leg back to place with the knee bent slightly, and touch the toe to the floor beside the right instep; then take three quick sidesteps (left, right, left) to the left (facing dancers will go in opposite directions). Each then should stand on the left foot, touch the right heel and toe, and sidestep (right, left, right) back into a line. (This is done twice.) Individual dancers sashay out of the line, hands joined with original corners, back to the starting lines, and face center.

CALL

Head (Side) Couples divide and step apart
Side (Head) Two Couples will quarter out

Sashay eight to the center of the set
Sashay back you're not through yet

Sashay eight to the center of the floor
Make a line we'll dance a little more

Heel and Toe, out you go
Heel and Toe, in you go

Heel and Toe, go out you do
Heel and Toe, back in with you

Sashay out you're doing fine
Turn a quarter around and make a line

All circle left around you go
Stop in place at home you know.

DIP AND DIVE (OVER AND UNDER): with California twirl, wrap
An old movement

When *Dip and Dive* is a three-couple movement it involves opposite couples and one other. A preliminary movement brings them into position with a couple in the middle facing an outside couple with another couple facing in behind them. The inside couple makes an arch with joined inside hands, and the outside couple facing them dives through and immediately makes an arch for the other outside couple, now facing them, to dive through. (Those facing out automatically California twirl.) The dipping and diving are repeated until all are back in original places. (An arm wrap movement may be substituted for the California twirl when the couple facing out reverses the direction faced. With inside hands joined and held at waist level, the lady turns back left face until her own arm encircles her waist as the gent walks behind her and turns right face to stand with his right arm around her. After diving through, he pulls gently to roll the girl out to position to make an arch.)

For a four-couple *Dip and Dive* movement there are two sets of facing couples. Each couple joins inside hands, and opposites alternate making arches (over) and diving through (under) the arches. The designated (active) couples begin by diving through.

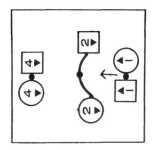

Position for starting dip and dive.

CALL I

First (Second, Third, Fourth) Couple right,
    circle half like thunder
Dip and Dive, don't you blunder

Inside high, the outside low
Dip and Dive, away you go

Dip and Dive across the track
Dip and Dive a-comin' back

When you get 'em straight home you go
Swing your own around just so.

CALL II

All promenade around the town
Head (Side) Two Couples wheel around

Side (Head) Couples arch, *Heads (Sides)* go
    under
Dip and Dive twice, you go like thunder

Head (Side) Couples wheel around
All promenade to your hometown.

LADIES (GENTS) BACK-TO-BACK
This is a modified version of an old figure dance

"Ladies center, back-to-back. Gents run around the outside track . . ."

From home positions, couples join inside hands, and the designated persons (ladies, gents) are led to the center to stand back-to-back and face partners. The partners left in home position turn and promenade (ccw) outside all the way around them, skip partners, swing the next, and promenade to the gents' home positions.

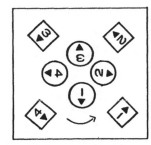

"Ladies to the center back-to-back. Gents go around the outside track . . ."

CALL

Ladies (*Gents*) to the center *Back-to-back**
Gents (*Ladies*) dance around the outside track

Don't you tease, don't you vex
Skip your partner, swing the next

Take that lady, promenade all
Promenade eight around the hall

Promenade as pretty as you can
Promenade home with your new man, and . . .

*Repeat the entire dance three more times.

QUARTER SASHAY (FORWARD SIX, FALL BACK EIGHT)
An old figure dance

The *Quarter Sashay* as used here calls for those designated to move sideways (sashay) to the right a quarter around the square to the next couple position (i.e., from the position of Couple 1 to the position of Couple 2).

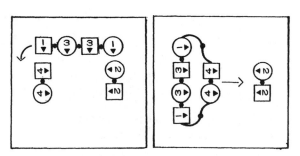

"Quarter sashay to the right . . ."

". . . and forward six . . ."

CALL

First Couple* bow and swing
Go down the center and split the ring

Lady go gee, gent go haw (separate)
Around one and line up four (join hands)

Forward four and fall back four
Quarter Sashay four to the right
(Stand behind Couple 4; at the ends of the lines, Gent 1 joins a hand with Lady 4, Lady 1 with Gent 4)

Forward six and fall back eight (Couple 2 follows)
Forward eight and fall back six (Couple 2 stays in place)

Quarter Sashay four to the right (to Couple 1 position)
Forward four and fall back four

Sashay four to the right
(Stop back of Couple 2; ends of each line join hands)
Forward six, fall back eight (Couple 4 follows to center)

Forward eight, fall back six (Couple 4 stays in place)
Sashay four to the right

Forward four and circle four
In the middle of the floor

Break it up with a do paso
Partner left, corner with the right
Grab your honey and home you go
Everybody swing.

*Substitute, in turn, *Second Couple*, *Third Couple*, *Fourth Couple*, and make appropriate changes in the dancers designated in the parentheses.

RIP AND SNORT
THREAD THE NEEDLE

These are old movements used primarily as endings to dances or exhibitions

For *Rip and Snort,* with all hands joined in a circle, the designated couple dances forward toward an arch made by their opposite couple. As they go under the arch they (only) drop hands with each other, separate, and go around opposite directions back to each other, those behind them following through the arch. The arching dancers turn toward each other and follow the others through their own arch. The lead couple rejoins hands, ending with all back in a circle.

"*Heads down the center, rip and snort . . .*"

"*Go through the arch and cut 'em short . . .*"

"*Couple No. 3 wring the dishrag . . .*"

"*All circle left again . . .*"

"*Heads down the center, rip and snort . . .*"

The end result of the *Thread the Needle* movement is to have all dancers in a line facing an audience with all hands joined (except those on the ends) and crossed in front of the dancers. All dancers join hands and circle until Gent 3 and Lady 2 (corners) have their backs to the audience. Gent 1 and Lady 4 (corners) start a rip and snort through an arch between Gent 3 and Lady 2 by separating, gent going right, lady left, and each pulling other dancers in their end of the line through the arch. Dancers in the arching couple turn (toward each other) and face the audience, their arms crossed in front of them. Gent 1 leads through an arch between Gent 2 and Lady 2, while Lady 4 leads through an arch between Gent 3 and Lady 3. Lady 3 and Gent 2 turn around to face the audience with arms crossed. Gent 1 leads through an arch between Gent 2 and Lady 1, while Lady 4 leads through an arch between Lady 3 and Gent 4. Lady 1 and Gent 4 turn around to face the audience with arms crossed. Gent 1 and Lady 4 turn and face the audience with arms crossed. All bow from the waist, then in unison each lifts the still joined arm that is on top over his head, turn to face in, and all circle or California twirl and promenade.

CALL I

All circle to the left don't you fall
First (Second, Third, Fourth) Couple Rip and Snort go down the hall

Couple up hands and circle around
Stop in place in your hometown.

CALL II

All circle left keep time to the fiddle
First Gent and *Fourth Lady, Thread the Needle* in the middle

Loop back through, between the next two
Take another stitch go under and through

Turn right around, stand in a straight line
Bow to the folks you're doing fine

Lift arms up high and straighten the line
California twirl, promenade so fine.

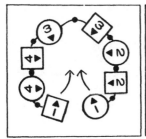 

"Thread the needle . . ."
While circling, the lead couple breaks the handclasp between them and moves forward toward an arch made by the opposite couple.

They pull the line of dancers behind them through the arch, separate, and go around the outside back to place. The arching dancers reverse the direction faced and stand with arms crossed in front of them.

ARKANSAS TRAVELER
Adaptation of an old figure dance

This figure is made up of a series of turn throughs that are self-explanatory in the call. It can include an innovation if each promenade only moves dancers up to the next position. This is called a "quarter promenade."

CALL

Heads* (Sides) go forward and come on back
Turn through opposites across the track

Turn partners with a left hand around
Corners with the right, right all around

Partners left, left all around
Turn corner with the right, Promenade a quarter around.

*Dance four times with those in head positions leading, then four times with those in side positions leading.

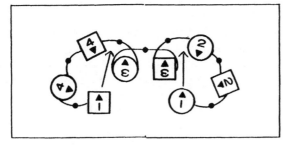

The lady then goes right, through an arch made by the couple at her right,

and the gent goes left through an arch made by the couple at his left.

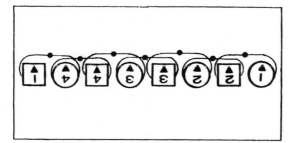

When all other dancers have reversed directions,

the lead dancers turn to place in line with them.

TEACUP CHAIN

A beautiful figure dance of the forties often presented in exhibition

This is a complicated movement that starts with all dancers in home positions and must be memorized, as there is no specific directive call for it. It was worked out by Mrs. P. M. Lewkowicz of Austin, Texas, who used teacups for dancers. It is very pretty when ladies hold skirts out at sides while dancing.

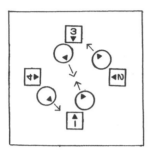 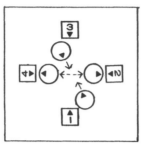

Head gents receive ladies from side gents for a courtesy turn. *Side gents receive ladies from the center for a courtesy turn.*

Ladies only do a series of stars and courtesy turns. *Gents stay in place and courtesy turn the ladies* with the left or right hand (left arm around her waist), according to which hand she offers him (sometimes using the same hand twice in a row). Ladies alternate right and left hands. Head Ladies start with right hands, Side Ladies with standard courtesy turn. Head gents always receive new ladies from the gents at their left and send them to the center. Side gents receive new ladies from the center and send them to the gents at their right. For easier learning, head and side ladies should first practice separately, then simultaneously.

Head Ladies
1. Star right three quarters around in the center.
2. Left hand (ccw) courtesy turn with side (corner) gents.

3. Right-hand (cw) courtesy turn with head (opposite) gents.
4. Left-hand star one and a quarter times around in the center.
5. Right-hand (cw) courtesy turn with other side gent.
6. Left-hand (ccw) courtesy turn with heads (original partner).

Side Ladies
1. Right-hand (cw) courtesy turn with head (corner) gents.
2. Left-hand star one and a quarter times around in the center.
3. Right-hand (cw) courtesy turn with side (opposite) gents.
4. Left-hand (ccw) courtesy turn with head gents.
5. Right-hand star three quarters around in the center.
6. Left-hand (ccw) courtesy turn with sides (original partners).

CALL

Allemande left as pretty as you can
Courtesy turn your ladies in a *Teacup Chain*

Any fill-in patter may be called during the dance, such as:

Head Ladies star in center, *Side Ladies* to head gents
Dance as pretty as you can, hold skirts out wide

Side Gents take 'em from the center
And send 'em to the heads

Head Gents turn 'em around then to center they go
Dance the *Teacup Chain*, on a heel and toe

Make courtesy turns and stars you know
When you get back home turn in place just so.

IV
ROUND DANCING
AND
CONTRA DANCING

The New Look of Round Dancing

"Tradition tells us that in 1830 a little Bohemian peasant girl by the name of Anna Slezak had an inspiration one summer afternoon and began making up a little tune in her head, while she skipped around in step with its catchy rhythm. Delighted with it, she made words to her tune, and danced and sang to her heart's content. Joseph Neruda, the schoolmaster, happened to pass by and he was just as delighted, so he wrote down the words and the melody of her little song and in the next week had his students and village girls all perform the new dance in their home village of Elbeteinetz.

"It was catchy. It spread. Within a few years they were dancing it in Prague, where they gave it the name Polka, from the Bohemian word *pulka,* which means half, and refers to the little half step or close-step that was characteristic of it. Under this new name it soon appeared in Vienna. By 1840 a dancing master of Prague took it for exhibition to the Odeon in Paris, and it immediately found its way into every dancing salon.

"The Polka was introduced into the ballrooms of France and England in 1843 and led to the inauguration of the present style of round dancing." (Shaw, *The Round Dance Book*)

The term "round dancing" has been applied to ballroom dancing as performed by couples who freely choose their own pattern of steps to varied rhythms such as two-step, waltz, polka, or rumba, and also to early-day stately stylized European dances with set patterns, such as the minuet. American round dances are a unique combination of the two, with the addition of a leader who "cues" the movements while the dancers are performing them.

This type of round dancing grew out of the great surge of interest in square dancing that began in the forties and is still going strong. Widening interest and the production of masses of choreographed round dances of increasing complexity led to the organization of clubs restricted to round dancing, yet "rounds" remain an important part of the square dance picture. Since many square dancers do not spend a great deal of time round dancing, some of the rounds with simpler choreography have been selected and designated "square dance rounds." Very often experienced round dancers meet and dance more complicated routines in the hour immediately preceding the actual beginning of a square dance. Round dance costumes are the same as those for square dancing.

Mixers are rounds choreographed so that dancers are constantly changing partners. Icebreakers are simple, traditional, or modern dances designed to get the dance started smoothly with simple choreography that everyone can dance with ease. Some dances have dual choreography, allowing them to be danced either as rounds or mixers, and some dances serve as both mixers and icebreakers.

Beginning the evening with the Grand March (an icebreaker) gets everyone into position for square dancing without their having to start the evening hunting for a place in a set. Interspersing a few mixers in the program of square dances promotes friendliness and helps people get to know each other better, especially when they keep the last change of dancers as partners for the next square dance tip. The inclusion of rounds in a square dance program not only helps provide a more balanced program, but the extra training in disciplined rhythmical movements also results in smoother, more graceful square dancing.

Each round dance is a series of movements, called a routine, designed into a set pattern for a particular piece of music. Couples follow each other around a circular pattern, each dancing the routine at the same time.

The most frequently used rhythms are the two-step (duple time) and the waltz (three-quarter time). Many popular tunes are used as bases for round dance routines. A few of these dances maintain their popularity through the years and are considered "classic dances," the same as "Stardust" is considered a classic American melody. For 1974, the list of classics (with the name of the author and the record label and number) included: "In The Arms of Love" (Morrison), Decca 32034; "Dream Awhile" (Ellis), Mercury 30004; "Moon over Naples" (Brownyard), Decca 31812; "Three A.M." (Moss), Decca 31778; "Neapolitan Waltz" (Harden), Windsor 4626, Grenn 14003; "Lazy Quick Step" (Moss), Mercury 71307X45; "Dancing Shadows" (Arnfield), Windsor 4682; "Feelin'" (Barbee), RCA Victor 47-9689; "Spaghetti Rag" (Gniewek), Hi-Hat 831; "Kon Tiki" (Glazier), Mayflower M-19; "Mexicali Rose" (Stapleton), Grenn 14210; "Green Door" (Procter), Belco B-207; "Somewhere, My Love" (Wylie), Columbia 33104; "Let's Dance" (Stone), Hi-Hat 803; "Birth of the Blues" (Parrott), Decca 29360. Another longtime favorite is "Miss Frenchy Brown" (Harue and Marge Tetzlaff), Grenn 14182; and a popular Latin rhythm classic is "Tango Mannita" (Manning and Nita Smith), Grenn 14198. When ordered from square and round dance sources, these records come complete with "cue sheets."

Cue sheets for seven classics that are in the "square dance rounds" category are given in the section on Selected Round Dances. They are: "Dancing Shadows"; "Mexicali Rose"; "Birth of the Blues"; "Tango Mannita"; "White Silver Sands"; "Left-footers' One-Step"; and "Miss Frenchy Brown." Also included are a selection of other rounds and mixers, some adapted from traditional dances.

The dances selected are presented in standard round dance "cue sheet" form, which includes the name and label of the record for which the dance was written and the "cue" words to be given by the leader. Current sources for other records with cue sheet instructions are advertized in the magazines listed near the end of this book under "Bibliography and Sources of Other Material."

Explanations of terminology and symbols used in round dancing, and directions for performing the basic steps, are explained under the headings of: "How to Read a Round Dance Cue Sheet"; "Round Dance Terms: Selected Definitions"; "Steps and Figures"; "Round Dance Positions"; "Round Dance Symbols and Abbreviations"; and "American Round Dance Rhythms." The explanations are those most popularly used in today's round dancing.

How to Read a Round Dance Cue Sheet*

"To most people, the initial glance at a cue sheet is like reading something in a foreign language. It takes a little time and patience to learn to interpret one quickly. Here are a few explanations which may be of some help.

"If all instructions for a dance were written out in full, most cue sheets would be several pages long, so abbreviations are used. Where we normally use a period (.) to signify an abbreviation, there are no periods used for this purpose in round dance cue sheets. That is, if

we were to use the abbreviation for Line of Dance (the usual method of taking the first letter of each word follows through here), it would not be printed L.O.D. but, instead, LOD—no periods and all run together. In the same way OP stands for Open Position; even more peculiar looking are the words SCAR (Side-car).

"A measure is a set number of beats or counts in music and each piece of music has this set number of counts per measure throughout. Two-steps most frequently have four counts to a measure, while waltzes usually have three. In round dance cue sheets these measures are grouped in lots of four. Therefore, you will notice when you pick up a cue sheet that the measures are listed 1–4, 5–8, etc.

---

* The following excerpts were taken with permission from a booklet written by Alf and Elisabeth Evans, Burnaby, British Columbia, Canada, as a reference guide to their course in round dance basics. The excerpts are reprinted through the courtesy of *Canadian Dancers News*.

This method breaks your measures down into useable sections.

"Punctuation also plays a large part in your cue sheet. Each punctuation mark has a special significance. First, the comma (,) indicates that the movement described before it takes one beat or count to execute; next, the dash (−) means a *hold,* one of the most difficult things to accomplish because you do nothing for that count; thirdly, the semicolon (;) which denotes the end of a measure; fourth, the slash (/) which marks a split measure or count; lastly the parenthesis (), used as a preface to the footwork for a familiar movement. For example: Limp (Side, Behind, Side, Behind;).

"All cue sheets are written with directions given for the man. Footwork is for him and, unless otherwise stated, the lady must use the opposite foot.

"All cue sheets have their directions written twice; once in the "cue line" describing the footwork and sometimes the position; then in fine print below giving the movement in detail. Most record companies are now numbering the measures in fine print which makes them easier to follow.

"You must be very thorough in checking the fine print as sometimes it includes special directions for the lady which are not included in the cue line. Also it is here you find your facing position, the specific direction of a certain movement such as a twirl, wheel, and your dance position.

"Let us use a few examples to illustrate what we have said before. Here are the first four measures of the classic, Dancing Shadows: *Walk, −, 2, −; (Scissors) Side, Close, Cross, −; Side, Close, Back, −; Bwd Two-Step;* This allows us to use many of the things referred to in the above paragraphs.

"When learning a dance you should never go further than about four measures at one time. Become familiar with these, then add four more and build your dance in this manner. You will notice that there are four semicolons so we know that this description covers four measures; that the two *Walk* steps are slow with a *Hold* after each (see the dashes?); that the "Scissors" step is emphasized in parenthesis; that the abbreviation *Bwd* is used for "backward"; that a two-step requires one four-count measure to execute. All of this you learn from the cue line described above, but you must refer to the fine print for your detailed footwork and direction of movement.

"Just think! A two-step can be done in LOD, RLOD, to the WALL, to COH, and diagonally between all of these; but in the cue line it would just be written *Fwd Two-Step!*

"Similarly, it could be done in Open, Closed, Semi-Closed, Left-Open, Half-Open, Banjo or Sidecar Position, etc. The man could walk while the lady twirls, rolls, or executes some other different movement.

"If you take the time to decipher a cue sheet and work it out carefully, you will find that it becomes as clear as your daily newspaper."

Round Dance Terms: Selected Definitions

As round dancing expanded from simple dances of earlier times to the complicated modern dances now popular, a more extensive vocabulary of terms evolved and was standardized. Here is a selected list of these terms based on material used by permission from Norman and Helen Teague's *Manual for the Round Dancer.*

Break A short figure between the parts of a dance or between repetitions of a dance.

Sometimes called a "bridge" or "interlude."

Clockwise Movement in the direction of the hands on a clock. Reverse line of dance around the hall.

Counter-clockwise Movement in the opposite direction of the hands on a clock. Line of dance around the hall.

Counterpart Steps or figures executed by one partner at the same time the other partner is doing his or her part.

Count(s) A beat or beats of music.

Couple Dancing partners.

Cues Abbreviated instructions, written or spoken to help dancers remember a routine. Cues are ordinarily directed to the man, with the woman doing the counterpart unless the cue word or words are used to indicate both parts.

Diagonal(ly) Oblique, at an angle.

Ending The last steps, figure, or position taken at the end of a dance. Also see *Tag*.

Figure A definite sequence or series of steps forming one part of a dance routine.

Free Hand The one not in contact with the partner.

Free Foot The one not bearing the weight, usually used for the next step.

Hold A specified number of counts when no step is taken. Sometimes used to indicate contact in a dance position.

Inside Hand or Foot The one nearest partner when standing side-by-side.

Introduction A short dance figure preceding the main part of a dance routine.

Lead-in Music played before the introduction or dance figure begins.

Lead or Leading The act of directing a partner in the performance of a dance by body contact. Usually the man's role.

Leading Hand or Foot The forward hand or foot in relation to the direction of movement. May indicate the starting foot.

Left Refers to the left hand or foot. May be used to indicate direction.

Line of Dance Counterclockwise direction around the hall.

Measure(s) A bar or bars of music.

Mixer A term used to indicate that partners are exchanged during the course of the dance routine.

Opener Same as introduction.

Opposite Used to indicate opposite footwork, each partner doing a counterpart movement of feet (or hands); for example, as one partner's left foot steps forward, the other partner's right foot moves backward. May also refer to direction.

Outside Hand or Foot The one farthest from the partner when standing side-by-side.

Phrasing The fitting of the steps of a dance to the four or eight measures of the standard musical phrase.

Position Any of the standard positions taken by a couple in dancing. See the section on positions.

Reverse Line of Dance Clockwise direction around the hall.

Rhythm In music the count of a measure, and in dancing the step count of the pattern or figure.

Right Refers to the right hand or foot. May be used to indicate direction.

Routine A series of steps or figures blended into a complete dance.

Run A fast series of steps taken without closing the feet together.

Same (Foot) Indicates same footwork or foot. Each partner moving the right or left foot at the same time. Synonym for identical.

Slowly Indicates a slower movement than normal for the tempo of the dance.

Solo Individual movement. Partners execute a step or figure separately.

Starting Position Position taken by a couple at the beginning of a dance or at the start of any figure in the dance.

Styling Individual execution of position or movement, which is used to enhance the appearance of the dance.

Supporting Foot The foot bearing the weight at the moment.

Trailing The hand or foot not executing the lead movement.

Tag A series of steps used at the end of a sequence or dance to utilize extra measures.

Tempo The rate of speed at which music is played.

Steps and Figures

Acknowledge Courteous recognition of partner, performed as dance directions indicate.

Across A term used to indicate movement from one side to the other.

Apart and Together Movement away from and back to partner *without* progression.

Away and Together Movement away from and back to partner *with* progression.

Back Opposite to direction faced.

Back-to-Back Partners travel along line of progression, turning away from each other to a full or partial back-to-back position.

Balance A "step, touch" and/or "hold" in the direction indicated, holding the weight on that foot for one or more counts.

Behind A step in back of the supporting foot. May also be used as a synonym for "in back of," indicating that one partner crosses in back of the other to change sides.

Bow and Curtsy A traditional ending in American round dancing: M's R & W's L hands are joined as they face each other. M bows toward his partner, bending at the waist. W "curtsies," keeping the upper part of her body erect as she points one foot in front of the other and bends the knee of the supporting leg to lower the body. She may or may not bow her head.

Box A series of steps so executed as to form a square pattern. May be done singly or as a couple.

Brush The ball of the free foot is brushed lightly on the floor in the indicated direction, without taking weight.

Buzz Step A spot turn by the dancer with weight on the supporting foot while pushing with the free foot to propel himself around. May be done singly or as a couple.

Canter A series of steps peculiar to waltz rhythm allowing only two changes of weight per measure. The weight changes are made on the first and third counts.

Change Feet The act of transferring the weight from one foot to the other.

Change Sides Partners exchange places.

Chasse (Sashay) A figure that involves a sideward movement in the direction indicated, with a series of "side, close" steps.

Check Step A transition maneuver in which a definite "stop" is executed just prior to reversal of direction or movement.

Chug To check a forward, backward, or sideward action by dropping the heels, bending the knees, holding the weight, and sliding the feet in the indicated direction.

Circle A figure in which a ring formation is executed.

Close Step A step in which the free foot is brought close to or beside the supporting foot to take the weight.

Corté A figure requiring a deep dip back for one partner and a dip forward for the other while partners are in closed position. In an "open corté," both partners dip back in a deep dip while in open position. (See *Tango Rhythm* under American Round Dance Rhythms)

Cross To move the hand or foot, from one side to the other of the opposite hand or foot; or move to the other side of the partner.

Cross Through The free foot moves in toward partner and between the couple as it is crossed in front of and beyond the supporting foot to take the weight, while the body follows through.

Cut Step Displacement of one foot by the other by hooking the free foot across, in front of, or in back of and to the side of the supporting foot so closely as to require the supporting foot to be drawn away.

Dip A step in the indicated direction, on the designated foot with a definite bend of that knee.

Draw Movement of the free foot up to the supporting foot, grazing the floor with the ball of the moving foot as that toe points away from the supporting foot with no weight change.

Face or Facing Indicates the direction toward which the front of the body is turned.

Face-to-Face Opposite of back-to-back. (See *Back-to-back.*)

Flare The free foot swings forward, out to the side, and to the rear; or out to the side and forward of the supporting foot, in a circular motion. Dance directions indicate a "backward" or a "forward" flare.

Flare Through A figure wherein a "forward flare" is combined with a cross through.

Grapevine A series of steps taken where "side steps" are followed by alternately crossing the free foot in back of or in front of the supporting foot. Variations of this figure are sometimes called a "strolling" or "twisty" vine, where partners change from banjo to sidecar position or vice versa as one partner crosses in back while the other crosses in front.

Hitch A series of steps in which the forward step is followed by a close, then a step back is taken with the free foot; or, a step back is followed by a close, then a step forward is taken with the free foot.

Hook A movement where the free foot crosses in front of and closes to the other side of the supporting foot to share the weight as an individual pivot is executed.

Hop To jump or spring lightly on the supporting foot to land again on the same foot.

In Used in two ways: to indicate direction toward the center of the hall, or to approach or face toward partner.

Kick A forceful extension or swing of the free leg.

Lift A movement where the free foot and lift are extended in an action similar to the swing, except that in the lift, the elevation is usually provided by straightening the flexed knee of the supporting foot and raising up on the ball of that foot.

Limp Action where the free foot moves in the direction indicated and beyond the supporting foot to take the weight as both knees are slightly bent.

Lock A figure where one step is followed by a second step in which the free foot crosses in front of or in back of and to the other side of the supporting foot to take the weight so closely as to require the supporting foot to move away. Movement may be forward or backward.

Lunge Sudden forward or sideward movement with the forward knee bent as the weight is taken. During this action both feet remain on the floor.

Maneuver (Blend) A term indicating a change of weight balance or body position, which is done in such a way as to smoothly blend one step or figure of a dance with the next.

On Indicates movement that continues in line of progression.

Open out Action in which partners change from a more "closed" position to a more "open" one.

Out Indicates direction toward the wall.

Polka A lively dance done to music in 2/4 time in which a Hop on Count 1 is followed by a two-step. Sometimes the Hop is done on Count 4.

Pas de Basque A figure where a step to the side on one foot is followed by a step on the other foot in front of the first, then a change of weight back to the first foot, in place. **Back Pas de Basque** A term sometimes used when the second step is taken behind instead of in front of the supporting foot. (See *Pas de Basque.*)

Pivot A turn involving rotation on the ball of the foot as each step is taken. May be done as a couple or as an individual.

Post Pivot A series of steps, done in closed position or loose closed position, where one partner marks time in place while the other crosses in front of him to his other side.

Reverse Pertains to line of dance indicating clockwise. When used with a twirl or spin, indicates a left-face twirl or spin.

Rock Transfer of weight from one foot to the other by stepping in the indicated direction on one foot, then shifting the weight back to the other in place.

Run A fast series of steps in line of progression taken without a close.

Schottische A series of steps done in 4/4 time characterized by three running steps followed by a hop on Count 4 on the foot used for the third step.

Scissors Twinkle A variation of the twinkle wherein partners move from sidecar to banjo position or vice versa. One partner executes the cross in back while the other crosses in front. This may be done in place or in progression.

Slide A gliding step with the feet remaining in contact with the floor as each step is taken.

Spin A quick solo spot turn on the ball of either foot.

Spin Maneuver A combination of a spin and a maneuver, where one partner executes the spin while the other maneuvers into proper position.

Spot Turn A turn without progression.

Stamp or Stomp Placement of the entire foot on the floor with a strong impact.

Star Action where partners rotate around each other with indicated hands joined in star position.

Stork Step One or more small hopping steps, done in place, where the free foot is lifted about an inch off the floor with the toe pointed out.

Sweep The free foot is moved away in the direction indicated (side, back), and to the front of the supporting foot keeping the toe touching the floor.

Swivel A change of direction and a change of position made while weight is on the ball of the foot.

Tamara A series of steps involving changes of hands and positions: Partner facing COH places L hand in back near his R hip; partner with back to COH reaches across with R hand to take partner's left hand, while the other hands are joined and arched above head level. The raised hands are freed as partners pass right shoulders to exchange places and turn to face each other, to repeat action if dance directions so indicate.

Tap A sharp, audible sound made by contacting the floor with the toe or sole of either foot.

Touch The toe of the free foot is touched to the floor in the position indicated, without taking weight as: near the instep of the supporting foot (in step-touch); forward; in back; or to the side.

Twinkle A series of steps involving a change of direction and a cross step: The free foot crosses in front of or in back of and beyond the supporting foot to take the weight as a partial body turn is made in the direction of the cross.

Twirl A turn made by the woman under her own and the man's joined, uplifted R or L hands. (Standard twirl is R face, or CW; reverse twirl is L face or CCW.)

Twist Movement of the feet where a turning motion from side to side is done with either the ball or heel of the foot. The weight may be on one foot or both feet.

Walk A series of steps in line of direction indicated, taken without a close, at a speed normal to a specific tempo.

Wheel A series of steps where partners turn as a couple, with one serving as a pivot or "hub," while the other moves in a larger circle around him. The term usually applies to positions other than closed, as when partners are side-by-side.

Wrap For the standard wrap, from side-by-side position with the lady at the man's right, inside hands are joined (M's R, L's L), these arms are extended as the lady makes a complete left face turn, at the same time wrapping the arms around her waist to end facing forward at the man's right side. Free hands are joined at chest height if directed. The wrap may also be executed with the lady at the gent's left side making a right-face turn with opposite hands joined; or from either side or from facing position with both hands joined. When both hands are joined, the arms not being wrapped are raised above the lady's head in an arch while she is turning.

Round Dance Positions

CLOSED

In this as in all positions, both partners must "dance tall," with the weight forward on the balls of the feet and with each partner supporting his own weight with a balanced and relaxed carriage.

Closed.

Partners face each other almost directly, with shoulders parallel. The comfortable execution of many dance steps is hindered by the tendency to habitually assume the off-center position of the banjo square dance swing or to dance with the shoulders in a "V" similar to that of semiclosed position. The man's right arm partially encircles the woman with his right hand, fingers together and straight but relaxed, in contact with her back just below the L shoulder blade (relative size of partners will determine actual placement of hands and

arms). His right arm is held horizontally, with the elbow pointing to the side rather than toward the floor. The woman's left arm rests along the length of the man's right arm—contact near the elbow is especially important. Her left hand lies along the back and top of the man's upper arm or shoulder. Partners must maintain a definite and even resistance or "apart pressure" between the man's right hand and the woman's back, all along the encircling arms, and between the woman's left hand and the man's shoulder. It is through this contact and resistance that she can immediately feel any change of movement or direction made by the man's body and be effectively led through the figure. The man's left hand is held palm up at about the woman's eye height and well out to the side, with elbow curved rather than sharply angled. The woman's right hand rests palm down on his, and both keep fingers together and fairly straight. A tight, clutching clasp with heavy thumb pressure is especially to be avoided. The woman must bear her own weight and avoid hanging on the hand and arm of the man.

"Loose closed position," while not considered to be a standard hold, is an important variation in situations where a figure requires quick changes of direction or a crossing movement of the legs and feet. Partners merely stand farther apart while maintaining the same hand and arm positions and continuing to face each other.

PROMENADE

Partners face forward, side-by-side. Hands are joined right to right and left to left, with the right on top. The man's hands are held palm up; the woman's hands, palm down. Joined hands should be above waist level for good appearance. (See Promenade in Square Dance Section.)

Semiclosed.

Half open.

SEMICLOSED, REVERSE SEMICLOSED

Similar to the closed position in that hand positions are maintained, but partners turn so that each faces forward as they open out into a "V," with man's right and woman's left hips

adjacent and the joined hands extended forward at shoulder level. For reverse semiclosed position hand positions are adjusted so that partners open into a "V" facing RLOD.

SEMIOPEN (HALF OPEN)

A variation of open position, similar to closed in that the man's right arm encircles the woman's waist, and the woman's left hand rests lightly on his upper arm or lower shoulder. Partners stand side-by-side, both facing the same way as in open position, with their outside hands free (not joined), and these hands carried as described for open position.

ESCORT

Partners stand side-by-side both facing forward with the lady at the gent's right side. The woman's inside arm is passed through the crook of the man's inside elbow, with her hand resting on the man's wrist (individual styling finds some variation in hand placement). The appearance is that of "arm-in-arm." Free hands are held as in open position.

LEFT- (OR RIGHT-) HAND STAR

Partners face in opposite directions, with left hips adjacent, and left hands, palm to palm with fingers pointing up, held at about eye level. The rotation is done in this parallel position with dancers close enough to permit the forearms to maintain light contact. Free hands are held away from the body slightly above the waist for balance. Forearm grasps are sometimes used. (For right-hand star, reverse the directions.)

BUTTERFLY

Variation of facing position. The arms are held well out to the side at shoulder level or higher with palms facing and fingers pointed up. A similar hand and arm position is sometimes styled in banjo or sidecar position.

Reverse semiclosed.

Open.

Facing.

FACING

Partners face each other squarely, usually with the man on the inside facing the wall. Both hands are joined at about the woman's shoulder level and may be outstretched to the side or not, depending on the routine involved; the man's hands are held palm up, with the woman's hands placed palm down on them.

OPEN

Partners stand side-by-side, both facing forward. Inside hands are joined at the woman's shoulder level, with the man's hand palm up, the woman's palm down. The man's free hand should be held just above the waist away from the body for balance, palm out and fingers together, or near his body. The woman's free hand normally holds and flares her skirt.

BANJO

Same as closed position except that partners shift to stand with their right hips adjacent while maintaining hand holds approximately the same as in closed position.

SIDECAR

The opposite of banjo. Partners stand as in closed position but with left hips adjacent.

VARSOUVIANNA

Partners stand side-by-side, both facing forward with the lady at the gent's right side. The lady holds up both hands, palms forward, just higher and to the side of her shoulders. The gent clasps her hands in his by extending the left to her left across his chest, and the right to her right around her shoulders, all fingers pointing upward.

Banjo.

Sidecar.

Varsouvianna.

Round Dance Symbols and Abbreviations

(From *Round Dancer* magazine)

CP   Closed position

SCP   Semiclosed Position

OP   Open position

PT   Point

Ptr   Partner

Tch   Touch

Fwd   Foward—usually a progression in LOD —or to face fwd

Bk   Back—to step back, or to indicate, for example, M's bk to COH

LF   Left face (to turn LF)

RF   Right face (to turn RF)

Bwd   Backward—to move backward

Grapevine   Step as described in Steps and Figures.

XIB   Cross in back or XRIB—cross R in back (cue sheet will specify ftwk)

XIF   Cross in front, or cross R in front (cue sheet will specify ftwk)

L   Left—could be L hand or L ft

R   Right—could be R hand or R ft

Ft   Foot (for example, point R ft)

Ct   Count (for example, hold one ct)

Swd   Sideward

Hgt   Height

Wgt   Weight

Manuv   Maneuver; to smoothly assume position for next pattern of dance.

Bfly   Butterfly—facing ptr with arms extended to side and palms touching

Bjo   Banjo position—ptrs stand together so that R hips are adjacent

Scar   Sidecar position—ptrs stand together so that L hips are adjacent

Intro   Introduction—introductory meas of music leading into dance pattern

Meas   Measures—2/4 time (2 cts); 4/4 time (4 cts); 3/4 time (3 cts)

W   Woman

M   Man

Tog   Together; to step together

LOD   Line of dance (or direction)—usually to face CCW around hall

RLOD   Reverse line of dance (or direction) —usually to face or step CW around hall

CW   Clockwise, or a movement in RLOD around hall, or a turning movement

CCW   Counterclockwise—the opposite of CW

Thru   Through—to step thru

Ack   Acknowledge—to face ptr and bow or smile while stepping apart

/   Symbol splitting a meas or ct (for example, step/close, step, step/close, step)

–   Dash, meaning a hold ct

;   Semicolon; indicates end of measure

,   Comma; divides measures into cts

M's   Man's (for example, M's L hand)

W's   Woman's (for example, Woman's R hand)

Twd   Toward (for example, to step toward LOD or together)

Pos   Position (for example, take Closed Pos)

Diag   Diagonal(ly); to face or move diagonally

COH   Center of Hall

Pas de Basque   Step as described in Steps and Figures.

Bal   Balance—a movement more or less in place

S   Slow—to indicate movement or kind of step (as in Latin rhythm)

Q   Quick—to indicate movement or kind of step (as in Latin rhythm)

Prog   Progress—to move either fwd or bk

Hitch   A change-of-direction step (for example, fwd, close, bk, –;)

Check   Also a change-of-direction step— either fwd or bk (for example, fwd, bk, bk, –;) to stop mvmt

1–4   Numbers at L hand of description indicate numbers of meas in pattern

Fac, fc   Face

Apt   Apart

American Round Dance Rhythms

WALTZ

NOTE: All cue sheets are written with directions given for the man's footwork. Unless otherwise stated, the lady uses the opposite foot and, if backing, steps in the opposite direction.

Basic Form of the Waltz

Waltz music is written in 3/4 time, three beats of music to a measure. The basic movement is Step, Step, Close, with a change of weight on each successive beat.

Forward (or Backward) Waltz Step

In the forward waltz the first step is forward, the second step is forward going beyond the first, and the third step is a "close," taking the weight on that foot. When in closed position, the gent waltzes forward and the lady does a backward waltz step by stepping backward on the foot opposite from that of the man. The normal cue is Forward, Forward, Close.

Waltz Turns

The basic waltz step is used in most waltz turns. Except for the "box waltz step" the turns should tend to progress forward from the starting direction faced. Most of the turn is accomplished on the first step, whether forward or backward. A smooth turn requires a pivoting action on the balls of the feet. Following are three types of waltz turns as done in closed position.

1. *Forward right waltz turn* (CW): On the first count of the first measure, the man steps forward with his right foot, turning right by toeing *out;* on the second count, he steps on the left foot beyond the right, continuing the turn by toeing *in;* and on the third count he closes the right to the left. This should take him halfway around. On the first count of the next measure, he steps backward with the left, toeing *in;* forward with the right, toeing *out;* and closes left to right, ending facing original direction.

2. *Backward right waltz turn* (CW): The man steps backward with his left foot, toeing *in;* backward on the right foot, toeing *out;* and closes left to right. This should take him halfway around. To complete the turn he steps forward with his right foot, toeing *out;* forward on the left foot, toeing *in;* and closes the right to the left, ending facing the original direction.

3. *Forward left waltz turn* (CCW): This is a reverse turn. The man steps forward with his left foot, turning left by toeing *out;* backward on the right foot, toeing *in;* and closes left to right foot. He should be halfway around. To complete the turn he steps forward on the right, toeing *in;* backward on the left, toeing *out;* and closes the right to the left, ending facing the original direction.

Box Waltz Basic

The box is a series of steps executed to form a square, and the waltz box requires two measures to complete it. This is not a progressive movement. Partners may or may not be in closed position. In the first measure the foot movement for the man is: left foot forward; right foot forward to the side of the left and a few inches away; left foot closed to right. In the second measure it is: right foot backward; left foot backward to the side of the right and a few inches away; right foot closed to left. If in closed position, the lady does the counterpart with opposite footwork.

Box Waltz Turn

A turn may be executed by combining the basic waltz movements with the box step. This is usually a left-face turn with little or no progression. Four measures are required to complete the turn.

Solo Waltz Turn

This is an individual movement done as facing or side-by-side partners turn away from each other and circle around to complete a full turn in two measures. Partners start with opposite and outside feet, using the same footwork as in the standard waltz turns.

Other Waltz Basics

The fundamental descriptions under the heading *Steps and Figures* are in general terms, and most of them can be adapted to waltz rhythm. These basic steps include the "grapevine," the "twinkle," and many others; the difference is in the rhythm of execution. Where used on cue sheets, the timing and rhythm are indicated.

TWO STEP

NOTE: All cue sheets are written with directions given for the man. Footwork is for him and, unless otherwise stated, the lady uses the opposite foot and, if backing up, steps in the opposite direction.

Basic Form of the Two-Step

Two-step music is written in 2/4, 4/4, and 6/8 time. The basic two-step is done to four counts or beats and is cued, "Step, Close, Step, Hold."

Forward (or Backward) Two-Step

The forward or backward two-step can be done from a variety of positions. The basic movement is used unless the dance directions specify otherwise. To two-step forward, the first step is forward, the second is a "close," and the third is forward, followed by holding the free foot in place for one count. To two-step backward, the procedure is reversed.

Two-Step Turns

The basic two-step is used in all the commonly used two-step turns. A smooth turn requires a pivoting action on the balls of the feet. Except for the "box type" all the turns should tend to progress. The following three types of turns may be done in closed or side-by-side position.

1. *Forward right two-step turn* (CW): The man leads forward with his right foot, turning right by toeing *out* on the first step. On the second count, the left foot closes to the supporting foot; on the third count he toes *out*

and steps backward with his right foot, then holds for the fourth count. He should be halfway around at this point. To continue, he leads forward with his left foot, toeing *in;* closes the right to the left, steps backward on the left; and holds, thus completing a right turn.

2. *Backward right two-step turn* (CW): The man leads backward with his left foot, turning right by toeing *in;* closes the right to the left; leads forward with his left, toeing *in;* and holds for the fourth count. He should be halfway around at this point. To continue, he leads forward with his right, toeing *out;* closes left to right; steps backward on the right, toeing *out;* and holds, thus completing a left turn.

3. *Forward left two-step turn* (CCW): The man leads forward with his left foot, turning left by toeing *out;* closes right to left; and follows through as in the other two turns to make a full left turn all the way around.

Box Two-step Basic

The box is a series of steps executed to form a square, and the two-step box requires two measures to complete a figure. This is not a progressive movement. The man leads sideward to the left with the left foot; closes the right to it; steps forward with the left; and holds for one count. During the second measure he steps to the right with the right foot; closes the left to it; steps backward with the right; and holds for one count, completing the box formation. Partners may or may not be in closed position. Footwork is opposite if in closed position but identical if side-by-side.

Turns to the right or to the left may also be made using the box two-step while in either closed position or solo. It would normally take four measures. On the third count the foot should be turned in the direction of the turn desired.

Abilene Two-step "Lift"

This is a regional version of the two-step which was at one time the only square dance step done in the Abilene, Texas, area. It is danced the same as the standard two-step, except that there is a pronounced "lift" of the free foot beginning on the third beat and holding through the fourth.

Solo Two-step Turn

This is an individual movement done by facing or side-by-side partners who turn away from each other and circle around to complete a full turn in two measures. Partners start with opposite and outside feet, using the same footwork as in the standard two-step turns.

Other Two-step Basics

The fundamental descriptions under the heading *Steps and Figures* are in general terms, and most of them can be adapted to two-step rhythm. These basic steps include the "grapevine," the "twinkle," and many others; the difference is in the rhythm of execution. Where used on cue sheets, the timing and rhythm are indicated.

TANGO

All cue sheets are written with directions given for the man. Footwork is for him and, unless otherwise stated, the lady uses the opposite foot.

Basic Form of the Tango

Tango music is basically the same as the two-step. The main difference in the two rhythms is the division of the count and the individual styling. The deliberate manner in which it is danced with its proud, smooth carriage and the quick and slow movements give the tango its special charm. The slow step is gliding and held long. It takes about one second and is given two beats of music. The fast ones are sharp and deliberate and taken exactly on the beat. In a two-step, the body and legs are in constant motion, stressing the follow-through. Although the same number of steps may be involved, the tango is danced more flat-footed with a complete change of weight on the stepping foot before releasing the other foot from the floor. Most of the basic figures and patterns can be adapted to the tango. Timing may vary. Dance instructions will indicate the specific timing and movements. Listed below are some of the basic figures used.

Promenade or Walking Step and Tango Close

Place one foot directly in front of the other and turn the toes slightly out. As the step is taken, bring the other one after it in a long, easy motion with "catlike" tread.

Figure 1

Fwd, –, Fwd, –; Fwd, Side, Draw, –;
S   S   Q   Q   S

In CP fac LOD, M take two fwd S Steps; one fwd Q, one side Q, then draw the L toe slowly to the R arch; (make side step small and do not "jump" into it). ("Tango close" means a "side draw.")

Figure 2

Side, –, Thru, –; Fwd, Side, Draw, –;
S   S   Q   Q   S

In CP fac LOD M step diag COH and LOD to modified Bjo pos, fwd R in modified Bjo pos, fwd Q L, side R, S draw in CP fc LOD.

Figure 3

Side, –, Thru (to semi CP), –; Turn, Side,
S   S   Q   Q

Draw, –;
S

In CP fc LOD M side L twd COH turning to semi CP step thru, M steps almost in place L pivoting 1/4 L F as W takes a long step around M to M R side, draw L to R (above fig may be repeated twd wall to complete a full turn).

Corté and Tango Close

There are many versions of the corté. The most common one is done in closed position. Care should be taken not to "jump" into dip, and each partner carries his own weight. Motion is smooth and deliberate.

Dip Bwd, –, Recover, –; Fwd, Side, Draw, –;
S   S   Q   Q   S

In CP fc LOD M dip bwd L toeing out twd COH bending L knee with R leg extended, the toe on the floor; torso is erect, with shoulders fc LOD. (W fwd R bending R knee. L leg is extended bk from the hip with L toe on the floor pointing twd the wall. W arches bk and looks over L shoulder. Arms arch to accommodate the dip.)

"Habenero" or Rocking Steps

All "rock" steps are done with the feet apart and remaining on the floor. They may be taken forward, backward, or to the side. Movement is a transfer of weight from one foot to the other, with a rocking motion controlled in the knees, so the body does not bounce. There are many variations of this figure. Some are:

Figure 1: Forward Rock

Fwd, Place, Fwd, –; Fwd, Place, Fwd, –;
Q   Q   S   Q   Q   S

In OP M step fwd L leaving R ft in place, Q return of wgt to R allowing only the ball of that ft to take the wgt, step slightly fwd S L. Repeat action starting with M R ft.

Figure 2: Rock Thru

Fwd, Place, Thru, –; Fwd, Place, Thru, –;
Q   Q   S   Q   Q   S

In LOD semi CP M step fwd L, return wgt to R in place fc ptr in LOD CP, step thru twd RLOD with S L to take wgt adj to rev semi CP; repeat action St M R ft fwd twd RLOD, returning to fc LOD semi CP. (As the "thru" step is taken, give a "push" to the mvt with that ft as the toe leaves the floor.)

Figure 3: Gaucho Turn

Turn, Place, Turn, Place; Turn, Place, Turn,
Q   Q   Q   Q   Q   Q   Q
Place;
Q

In CP fc LOD M steps fwd L twisting slightly and turning L, recovers on R ft in place, repeating this mvt three more times to complete the turn; takes two meas. (As M steps fwd L and turns with a slight twist, his R knee will be in bk of his L knee.)

CHA CHA CHA

Basic Form of the Cha Cha Cha

All cue sheets are written with directions given for the man. Footwork is for him and, unless otherwise stated, the lady uses the opposite foot.

The music of this rhythm is written in 4/4 time. The steps are short and peppy. The hands are kept at about elbow height for easy interchange. It is a relaxed dance that permits conservative figures in closed position and gay ones in the open breaks. There is a slight dipping action of the hips without body bounce. Many of the basic figures can be adapted to the basic step, the timing of which is usually: S, S, Q, Q, S; this, however, may sometimes vary.

Figure 1: Forward Basic (Open and Closed)

Fwd, Bk, Bk/Cha, Cha; Bk, Fwd, Fwd/Cha
S   S   Q Q   S   S   S   S   Q   Q
Cha;
S

In the CP or OP M step fwd L keeping R ft in place, return wgt to R, step Bk L/Q R and S L in place; repeat this with M taking first step Bk on R ft. (On the quick steps the feet do not "close," as in a two-step.)

Figure 2: Side Basic

Fwd, Place, Side/Close, Side; Fwd, Place,
S   S   Q   Q   S   S   S
Side/Close, Side;
Q   Q   S

In CP M step fwd L, recover to place on R, step side L/close R to L, step side L; repeat this mvt St M R ft.

Figure 3: Side Breaks

Side, Break, Place/Cha, Cha; Side, Break,
S   S   Q   Q   S   S   S
Place/Cha, Cha;
Q   Q   S

In CP M bk COH, M step side L, breaking to L OP M step bk R to fc RLOD, recover to place Q L/step in place Q R, step in place S L; repeat this figure M step side R, break to OP step bk L to fc LOD, recover to place QR/step in place Q L, step S R in place.

Figure 4: Chase Steps

These figures combine the Fwd and Bk basic with individual turns, and ptrs pursuing one another twd COH & twd the wall. These are done without body contact, and may vary in timing.

RUMBA

All cue sheets are written with directions given for the man. Footwork is for him and, unless otherwise stated, the lady uses the opposite foot.

Music of the rumba is basically the same in timing as the two-step, except in the two-step the weight change is immediate; in the rumba the foot is placed first; then the count is taken up to transfer the weight. The weight is balanced forward, the upper torso erect. The knees are close together but relaxed and bent slightly forward. Steps are small and taken on the balls of the feet, with the heels coming in contact with the floor on the completion of each step. The feet are kept parallel, with no toeing in or out except on the turns and breaks. Many combinations of basic figures may be used in this dance. Combinations of the "slow" and "quick" movements may vary, but the most commonly used pattern in this country is based on a "Q, Q, S, –;" or an "S, Q, Q, –;" timing.

Rumba Walk Forward and Back

Fwd, 2, 3, Hold; Fwd, 2, 3, Hold; Bk, 2, 3,
 Q Q S   Q Q S   Q Q S
Hold; Bk, 2, 3, Hold;
       Q Q S

In CP or OP, M step fwd QL, QR, SL –; repeat St R ft; M step bk QL, QR, SL –; repeat St R ft (the timing should not be rushed, to give the "hold" a full ct).

Rumba Side Basic

Side, Close, Side, Tch; Side, Close, Side, Tch;
 Q   Q   S   S   Q   Q   S   S

In CP M step side QL, close QR to L, step side S L, tch R to L; repeat St M R ft.

Rumba Box

Side, Close, Fwd, –; Side, Close, Bk, –;
 Q   Q   S   Q   Q   S

In CP M step side QL, close QR, step fwd SL, –; repeat mvt St M R ft.

Rumba Breakaway Left and Right

Side, Bk, Recover, –; or Side, Bk, Recover, Face, –;

In CP M stps side QL (releasing M's R & W's L hands) step QR behind L to L OP, recover in place on SL, – (as ptrs fc each other, change to M L & W R hands); M step side QR, step QL behind R to O P, recover on SR to fc. (This figure may be done in open or semiopen position also.)

SAMBA

All cue sheets are written with directions given for the man. Footwork is for him and, unless otherwise stated, the lady uses the opposite foot.

Samba music is written in 2/4 or 4/4 time, with a combination of quick and slow counts. The movement is slightly bouncy but with a soft, tilting motion, like a swing of a pendulum. Knees are bent on the slow count and straightened on the quick, in an "up-down" movement. As step is taken forward, body bends back; as step is taken back, body bends forward. Arms are held slightly up and out, more vertical than is usual. Legs have a "springy" action using knees, ankles, and feet. Many varied steps and figures may be used in this rhythm.

First Basic Samba Forward and Back

Fwd, Close, Place, –; Bk, Close, Place, –;
 S   Q   S   S   Q   S

In CP or OP M step fwd SL, step fwd closing QR to L, step in place SL, –; step bk SR, Close QL to R, step in place SR, –;

Second Basic Samba Box

Fwd, Side, Close, –L; Bk, Side, Close, –;
 Q   Q   Q   S   Q   Q

In CP, M step fwd SL, step side QR, close QL to R, –; step bk SR, step side QL, close QR to L, –;

On the fwd step, lean the body to the left; on the bk step, lean the body to the right.

Selected Round Dances, Mixers, and Icebreakers

Following are instructions and cues for some selected dances—rounds, mixers, and icebreakers. Some of them fall into more than one category.

GRAND MARCH
(Mixer, Icebreaker)

Music: Any good march or spirited music with a strong, steady beat.

There are many versions of the Grand March. For this one an even number of ladies and gents line up on opposite sides of the hall, gents at the caller's right, ladies at the left. (The dance may begin with couples lining up instead of single dancers.) All face toward the foot of the hall (away from the caller). When the music starts, dancers march to the foot of the hall and make a ninety-degree turn toward the center. When the lead gent and lead lady (or couples) meet, they make another ninety-degree turn and go as a couple down the center toward the head of the hall (toward the caller). As subsequent gents and ladies meet, they form couples and follow behind the lead couple. When the line of couples reaches the head of the hall, alternate couples make ninety-degree turns away from each other, first going right, second going left back to the sides. They then retrace the original route as couples. When couples meet in the center, they turn and go in lines of four down the center. Alternate fours go right and left, and around, then come down the center in lines of eight. (If a square dance follows, alternate lines move to either side of the hall and "square their sets.")

Although there is no set call for the Grand March, the caller usually calls out a few directions with fill-in patter during its performance. An example follows.

CALL

Take your places for the Grand March.

Line up now along the wall
Do the grand march, go down the hall

With the right foot up and the left foot down
Make that big foot jar the ground

Turn toward the center and make it neat
Buckle up two (four) when the two lines meet

Come down the center two (four) by two (four)
Promenade like you always do
Promenade right down the floor

First couple (four) right, second left around
Every other one go around the town

Hurry up, cowboy, don't be slow
You won't go to heaven if you don't do so

Promenade two and promenade four
Keep that calico off the floor

Meet in the center, buckle up eight
Make a line, keep it straight

Come down the center like you always do
When you're all in lines, then you're all through.

See GRAND MARCH diagrams on next page.

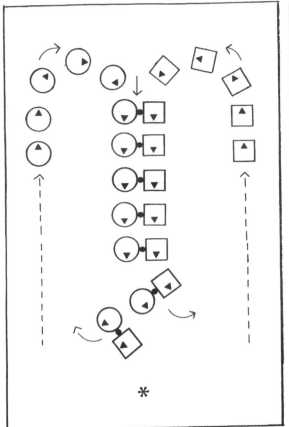

Grand march: "Down the center and buckle up two."

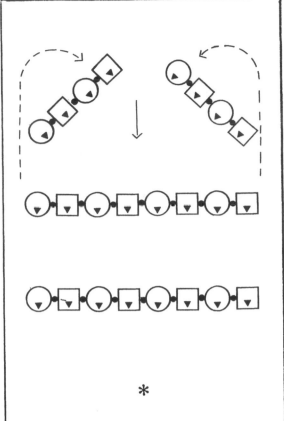

Grand march: ". . . make a line of eight and keep it straight . . ."

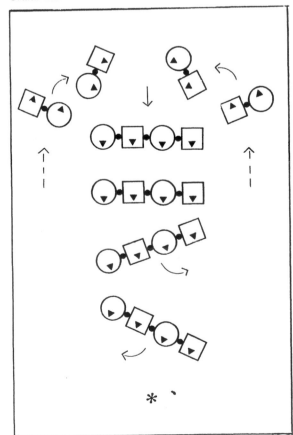

Grand march: ". . . come down the center four by four . . ."

PAUL JONES
(Mixer, Icebreaker)

Music: Any music with appropriate rhythm—waltz, polka, two-step, hocdown—and a strong, steady beat.

An even number of gents and ladies form two circles, one inside the other, with the gents in one, ladies in the other. Those in the inside circle join hands and face out; those in the outside circle join hands and face in. Adults usually have the men on the outside. When the music starts, each circle revolves to the left (they'll be going in opposite directions). Instead of using a call, at a given signal (the music is stopped briefly or a whistle is blown), the circles break, each dancer takes the person in front of him or her in the other circle as a partner and dances the appropriate steps together for a short time (waltz, two-step).

When the signal is repeated, they reform the circles and repeat the procedure, selecting a new partner. The procedure is repeated until the end of the music. When the signal is given for the dancers to take partners, a gent without a partner should assume responsibility for immediately finding any lady without a partner and dancing with her.

For Children: Unless they are well-trained dancers, instead of waltzing or two-stepping when dancing with partners, an easier dance is to promenade (in counterclockwise direction, boys on the left, girls on the right). Therefore, if the boys make the inside circle facing out and the girls make the outside circle facing in, there is less confusion leaving partners and getting back into circles. If a square dance is to follow, dancers may keep the last partners with whom they may dance it.

WHITE SILVER SANDS
(Mixer)

Composers: Manning and Nita Smith
Record: Jub. No. 5288, Grenn No. 15006
Position: Open, couples all facing LOD.
Footwork: Opp, M's L & W's R

Measures
1–4   *Walk, 2; 3, Turnaround; Bk up, 2; 3, 4;*

    Open pos, walk four steps fwd in LOD, doing an about face turning in twd ptr on fourth step; still traveling LOD walk bwd four steps;

5–8   *Repeat Action of Meas 1–4 in RLOD;*

9–12   *Bal Away; Bal Tog; Bal Away; Bal Tog;*

    Open pos facing LOD, pas de basque away from ptr stepping to side on L, step on ball of R ft in *front* of L, step in place on L, repeat starting with R ft for M (L for W);

13–16   *Turnaway, 2; 3, 4; Bal L; Bal R;*

    M turns away from ptr to his L (W turns R) in four steps, walks in small circle to take new ptr (W who was

behind his ptr); W moves to M ahead; face new ptr, join both hands, and bal to M's L (LOD) and then to his R.

    Start dance over with this new partner.

"PATTY CAKE POLKA"
(Mixer)

Traditional
Record: Windsor 4624 or any polka
Starting Position: Ptrs facing, both hands joined, M's bk twd center
Footwork: Opposite—steps described for M

Measures
1–4   *Heel, Toe; Heel, Toe; Slide, Two; Three, Four;*

    Strike L heel to floor diag out to L side, tch L toe to floor beside R ft; repeat; take four slide steps to L in LOD;

5–8   *Repeat Action of Meas 1–4 in RLOD, starting R ft;*

9–12   *Right Pat-Pat; Left Pat-Pat; Both Pat-Pat; Knees Pat-Pat;*

    Ptrs pat R hands tog three times; pat L hands tog three times; pat both hands tog three times; pat own knees with both hands three times;

13–16   *A Right-hand; Swing; and on; to the Next;*

    Ptrs hook R elbows and make one complete CW turn around each other with four steps starting with M's L ft; then M prog in LOD to next W with four steps starting L ft, while W prog in RLOD to next M with four steps starting R ft; new ptrs face, M's bk to center, join hands ready to repeat dance.

Repeat entire dance to end of music. The music for "Patty Cake Polka" is purposely arranged and phrased so that it may be used for almost any eight-, sixteen- or thirty-two-bar polka dance routine.

HEEL AND TOE POLKA
(May be used as a mixer)

Origin: Unknown
Music: "Little Brown Jug," or any polka
Position: Varsouvianna, with couples facing CCW in a circle
Start: Both with the left foot

Measures

1–2   Hop Two-Step left; Hop Two-Step right; Two polka-steps in LOD

3–4   Walk, 2; 3, 4; Four walking steps forward in LOD

5–6   Heel and Toe and the Lady Turn out; still in Varsouvianna position, both touch the left heel out to the side, touch the left toe to the floor beside the R foot. Release L hands, hold R hands, as the lady turns R face to RLOD with a two-step and the gent steps L-R-L in place. Both have wgt on L foot.

7–8   Heel and Toe; Lady Back up to Place; (or go to gent behind if for a mixer). Again a heel and toe as above, but using the right foot this time. The lady backs up to place, facing LOD, with one two-step, while the gent steps R-L-R in place. (For a Mixer, when the lady is facing RLOD, instead of backing up, she releases partner's hand and joins L hand with the gent in the couple following. He takes one two-step LOD as she takes one two-step in a left-face turn to become his new partner.)
Repeat all as many times as the music allows.

Variation: Lady twirls right face during the four walking steps.

BINGO WALTZ
(Mixer)

Record: Royal Canadian Record Co. RC I R, Bingo E-Z 2009
Dance Cues: Bill Castner
Steps: Waltz balance, roll away ½ sashay, step draw, walk.
Formation: Single circle of couples, facing center, hands joined woman on man's right.
This dance is suitable for teen-agers clear through "golden age" dancers.

Measures

1–4   *Balance In; Balance Out; Roll Away Half Sashay;*

1   Step on left foot to COH on Ct 1, bring right foot up to left on Ct 2 and hold Ct 3, while swinging joined hands forward during the balance in, do not put wgt. on right foot;

2   Step on right foot away from COH on Ct 1, bring left foot to right on Ct 2, hold Ct 3. Do not put wgt on left foot while swinging joined hands outward from COH;

3–4   Man rolls lady across in front of him (she makes a full left-face turn as he sidesteps to the right around the circle), and takes her right hand in his left during the roll to end in single circle again with her at his left side.

5–16   Repeat measures 1–4 three more times. At end of Meas 16, man faces LOD and lady on his right, while lady faces RLOD and him to take "butterfly" position, man's and lady's arms extended sideways—bodies about six inches apart.

17–24   *Step draw, Step draw (in), Step draw, Step draw (out) (Repeat)*

25–31   Still facing partners, take right hands and begin a "Grand Right and Left"; everyone shouts "B" while taking first right hand, "I" on taking left hand, "N" on right hand, "G" on left hand.

32   When meeting the fifth person, both hug and shout "Ooohh." (For children, or for other dancers who object to the hug, a swing—two-hand or square dance style—may be substituted.)

LEFT-FOOTERS' ONE-STEP
(May be used as a mixer)

Composers: Bruce and Shirley Johnson
Record: Decca No. 9-29558 or Windsor No. 4650, Grenn No. 15018
Position: SC, both facing LOD
Footwork: Opposite, steps described for M; nearly all movements start on M's L ft

Measures

1–2   *Walk, 2, 3, 4 (face); Side, Close, Side, Close;*

Start L ft and walk fwd in LOD four steps turning to face partner during the fourth step and taking closed dance position; step to L side in LOD on L ft, close R ft to L taking wgt on R ft, step again to L side in LOD on L ft, close R ft to L taking wgt on R ft while turning to face in LOD in semiclosed dance position;

3–4   *Repeat action of Meas 1 and 2,* except to end in closed position, M's back twd COH.

5–6   *Back in, 2, 3, 4; Side, Close, Side, Close;*

Start L ft and walk bwd twd COH four short steps; do two side-close steps in LOD, starting L ft as in Meas 2;

7–8   *Walk out, 2, 3, 4; Side, Close, Side, Close (to sidecar);*

Start L ft and walk fwd twd wall four short steps; do two side-close steps in LOD starting L ft as in Meas 2, except to end with L hips adjacent (sidecar pos), M facing RLOD and W facing LOD;

9–10   *Backward, 2, 3, 4 (face); Side, Close, Side, Close (to banjo);*

Start L ft and walk bwd 4 steps in LOD turning to face partner in closed position during fourth step; do two side-close steps in LOD starting L ft as in Meas 2, except to end with R hips adjacent (banjo pos), M facing LOD and W facing RLOD;

11–12   *Forward 2, 3, 4 (face); Side, Close, Side, Close (to semiclosed);*

Start L ft and walk fwd in LOD four steps, turning to face partner during the fourth step and taking closed position; do 2 side-close steps in LOD starting L ft as in Meas 2, ending in semiclosed position facing in LOD;

13–14   *Walk, Two Turn, Point; Walk, Two Turn, Point;*

Start L ft and walk fwd in LOD three steps, L-R-L, turning in twd partner to face RLOD during the third step, point R toe fwd to floor; start R ft and walk fwd in RLOD three steps, R-L-R, turning in twd partner to face LOD during the third step, point L toe fwd to floor;

15–16   *Two-step Fwd, Two-step Bwd, Twirl, 2, 3, 4 (to semiclosed);*

Start L ft and do a two-step "balance" fwd in LOD, start R ft and do a two-step "balance" bwd in RLOD; as M walks alongside with four steps starting L ft, W makes one R face twirl with four steps while progressing in LOD, to end with partners taking semiclosed position facing LOD, ready to repeat the dance. (If used as a "mixer," during Meas 16, W makes a four-step spot turnaway, turning R face to end about in same place started from, while M makes a four-step turnaway, turning L face twd COH to come alongside the next W in RLOD to gain a new partner.)
Perform entire dance a total of four times, ending with partners acknowledging after last twirl.

VARSOUVIANNA
("Put Your Little Foot")

Composers: Unknown
Record: HI-HAT No. 843, Windsor No. 4615-B
Position: Varsouvianna, Both facing LOD, wgt on R ft
Footwork: Identical throughout the dance
Intro: Wait two Meas.

Part A

Sweep/Glide, Close, –; Sweep/Glide, Close, –;
  1 Both starting with wgt on R and sweeping L up and across R dip R knee slightly and glide fwd in LOD on L, close R, hold 1 ct;
    Note: The "sweep" actually starts on the third beat of the measure before.
  2 Repeat the action of Meas 1;

Sweep/Glide, Close, Step; Point, –, –;
  3 Again sweep L up and across R dipping R knee slightly to glide fwd in LOD on L, close R, step fwd on L (both now have wgt on L ft);
  4 Point R ft fwd, hold two cts;

Sweep/Glide, Close, –; Sweep/Glide, Close, –;
  5–6 The action of these two measures is the same as in 1 and 2 *except* start with opposite foot (M's R & W's R).

Sweep/Glide, Close, Step; Point, –, –;
  7–8 Repeat Meas 3 and 4.
    Note: Repeat all of Part A before dancing

Part B

Sweep/Glide, Close, Step; Point, –, –;
  9–10 Same as Meas 3 and 4 in Part A.

Sweep/Glide, Close, Step; Point, –, –;
  11–12 Same as Meas 7 and 8 in Part A.

Sweep/Glide, Close, Step; Point, –, –;
  13–14 Same as Meas 3 and 4 in Part A.

Sweep/Glide, Close, Step; Point, –, –;
  15–16 Same as Meas 7 and 8 in Part A.

Ending

After completing Part B the last time through, drop hands and step apart on L to face ptr (M's bk to COH, W's bk to wall), M bows (head up) and W does a slight curtsy as music ends.

"JESSIE POLKA"

Composers: Unknown
Record: MacGregor No. 5001B, Blue Star No. BS-1588-A
Position: Two or more people standing in a line all facing LOD, arms around each other's waists.
Footwork—Same, both starting L

Introduction

Measures
1–4 *Wait, 2; 3, 4; 5, 6; 7, 8;*

Dance

1–2 *Heel (Fwd) Close; Toe (Bwd), Touch;*
  1 Bending only the R ankle and R knee joints tilt bwd touching heel fwd to floor L (while tilting bwd keep left leg, torso and head in a straight line as they were in the erect position), recover to the original erect pos with a close L (takes wgt);
  2 Bending only L ankle and L hip joints tilt fwd touching the free toe bwd to floor R (while tilting fwd keep the R leg, torso and head in a straight line as they were in the erect pos), again recover to the original erect pos but with a tch R (no wgt);

3–4 *Heel (Fwd), Close; Point Side, Point Fwd;**
  3 Repeat Meas 1 but heel (fwd) R, and close R (instead of using L ft);
  *Note: Meas 3 is done in some areas in erect pos with simply a KICK (Fwd) R, close R;

4 With left leg locked straight and toe pointed down, do a quick tap on the floor with the toe diag (LOD & COH) to side L, and repeat the tap fwd in front of supporting ft again with the L toe;

5–8 *Two-step Fwd; Two-step Fwd; Two-step Fwd; Two-step Fwd;*
    5–6 Prog LOD step fwd L/close R, fwd L; Fwd R/close L, fwd R;
    7–8 Repeat measures 5 thru 6;
Sequence: Twelve times through dance, plus ending

Ending

1–4 *Heel (Fwd), Close; Toe (Bwd), Tch; Heel (Fwd), Close; Point Side, Point Fwd;*
    1–4 Repeat Meas 1–4 of dance.

SCHOTTISCHE

Origin: Unknown
Music: Any schottische
Position: Half-open facing LOD, double circle
Footwork: Opp, M's L & W's R

Measures
1–4 *Walk, 2; 3, Hop; Walk, 2; 3, Hop;*
Half-open pos, walk three steps fwd LOD, hop after the third step, gent L-R-L-HOP, then R-L-R-HOP (lady opp foot).

5–8 *Bal Fwd; Bal Bk; Bal Fwd; Bal Bk;*
Take closed pos, step fwd LOD (M's L & W's R), touch opp toe beside fwd foot (M's R & W's L).
Repeat entire dance.
Alternate (may be adapted for Mixer):
Step turn Away, Hop; Step-Hop; Step-Hop; Tog-Step-Hop;
M turns away from ptr to his L (W turns R) in four step-hops rtn to ptnr (for mixer, gent moves up, lady back to next person in circle). Start dance over with original (or new) partner.
Repeat entire dance as many times as music allows.

HORSE AND BUGGY SCHOTTISCHE

Origin: Unknown
Music: Any schottische
Position: Two couples, open pos, facing LOD, one behind the other, two men's left hands joined, two women's right hands joined (lead couple reach bk, trailing couple reach fwd). Lead couple is in "horse" position, trailing couple in "buggy" position.
Footwork: Opp M's L & W's R

Measures
1–4 *Walk, 2; 3, Hop; Walk, 2; 3, Hop;*
With all hands joined, all walk three steps fwd LOD, step-hop after the third step, gent L-R-L-HOP, then R-L-R-HOP (lady opp foot)

5–8 Lead Two Turn Away
Step, Hop; Step, Hop; Step, Hop; Tog Step, Hop;
Keep all hands joined except lead couple, who release hands with each other (M's R, W's L). Lead M turns away from ptr to his left, lady turns right, and go around the trailing couple to meet and join hands behind them. Gent step-hops L-hop, R-hop, L-hop, R-hop. Lady step-hops, R-hop, L-hop, R-hop, L-hop. (Couples have now exchanged places.) Repeat entire dance as many times as music allows.

WALTZ OF THE BELLS

Composers: Doc and Winnie Alumbaugh
Record: Windsor No. 4605A
Position: Open dance pos, couples facing LOD, W on M's R, inside hands joined
Footwork: M & W use opposite footwork throughout; steps described are for the M

Part A

1–2 *Balance Forward, –, –; Balance Back, –, –;* Step fwd on L ft (Ct 1) while swinging joined hands fwd and up, tch R toe to side of and slightly in front of L ft (Ct

2, 3); step bk on R ft while swinging joined hands down and in bk (Ct 1), tch L toe to floor at side of R ft (Ct 2, 3);

3–4 *Balance Forward, –, –; and Back, –, –;* repeat action of Meas 1–2;

5–8 *Waltz, 2, 3; Turn, 2, 3; Slide; Slide;*
With joined hands still swung bk from Meas 4 above, start on L ft and take one waltz step fwd (L, R, L Ct 1, 2, 3); release hands, M makes a LF (CCW) turn with three steps while W makes a RF (CW) turn in three steps (Ct 1, 2, 3); end with ptrs facing and joining hands; then take two slide steps to M's L (CCW around room); step L, –, close R; step L, –, close R;

Part B

Repeat all of Part A, moving in opposite (CW) direction, starting with opposite ft (M's R and W's L).

Part C

1–2 *Slide; Slide;*
With both hands joined, ptrs take two slide steps to M's L (LOD);

3–4 *Twirl; Slide;*
M releases his L hand from W's R and takes one slide step to his L while W makes a RF turn with three steps (R, L, R) under her own L & M's R arms (Ct 1, 2, 3); join both hands and both take one slide step to M's L.

5–8 *Slide; Slide; Twirl; Slide;*
Repeat action of Meas 1–4 in RLOD, starting with opposite ft (M's R & W's L), with W turning CCW under her own R and M's L arm;

Part D

1–2 *Balance Away, –, –; Together, –, –;*
With inside hands joined (M's R & W's L), ptrs step (balance) away from each

other, M stepping bk on L ft, W bk on R ft; ptrs step fwd twd each other, M on R ft, W on L;

3–4 *Repeat Action of Meas 1–2 of Part D*

5–8 *Waltz, 2, 3; Waltz, 2, 3; Twirl; Now Ready;*
In closed dance pos take two waltzes (starting on M's L ft), rotating CW and progressing LOD around the room, making one complete turn; M drops R hand from W's waist and takes four steps in place (L-R-L-R), while the W makes a RF turn (CW) under her own R and the M's L arm with four steps (R-L-R-L). End by joining inside hands, both facing LOD ready to repeat the dance.
Repeat entire dance for a total of three times.

Note: To make this a "mixer" dance, W leaves her ptr as he releases her during the twirl on Meas 7–8 of Part D and advances to the next M ahead (CCW around the room).

After completing fourth cycle of the dance, use four meas ending of music by repeating first 2 meas of Part A (balance fwd and bk); then the W makes a RF turn under her own L & M's R arm on the third meas. Ptrs step away from each other at arm's length and bow deeply on fourth and final meas of ending.

"DANCING SHADOWS"
(Two-Step)

Composers: Edna and Gene Arnfield
Record: Windsor No. 4682
Position: Introduction, diag open-facing, dance, closed, M facing LOD
Footwork: Opposite throughout, steps described are for the M

Introduction

Measures
1–4 *Wait; Wait; Apart, –, Point, –; Tog, (to CP) –, Tch, –;*
Wait two meas in diag open-facing

pos, M's R and W's L hands joined; step bwd on L ft, hold one Ct, point R toe fwd twd ptr, hold one Ct; step fwd on R ft to face LOD taking CP, hold one Ct, touch L ft to R, hold one Ct;

Dance

1–4 *Walk, –, 2, –; (Scissors) Side, Close, Cross, –; Side, Close, Back, –; Bwd Two-step;*
Start M's L ft and take two slow walking steps fwd in LOD; (Scissors) M steps swd twd COH on L ft, close R ft to L, step on L ft XIF of R, (W XIB), hold one Ct; step swd twd wall on R ft, close L ft to R, step bwd in RLOD on R ft adjusting to CP M facing LOD, hold one Ct; (bwd two-step) M steps bwd in RLOD on L ft, close R ft to L, bwd again on L ft, hold one Ct;

5–8 *Bwd Two-step; Dip, –, Recover, –; Turn Two-step; Turn Two-step;*
Repeat action of Meas 4, starting M's R ft; in CP dip bwd in RLOD on L ft, hold one Ct, recover fwd on R ft maneuvering slightly R face, hold one Ct; start M's L ft and do two RF turning two steps progressing down LOD making a ¾ turn to end in CP M facing LOD;

9–16 Repeat action of Meas 1–8 ending in semiclosed pos facing LOD;

17–20 *Walk, –, 2, –; Point Fwd, –, (Hitch) Back, Close; Fwd, –, Thru, –; Vine, 2, 3, 4;*
Start M's L ft take 2 slow walking steps fwd in LOD; point L toe fwd in LOD, hold one Ct, (Hitch) step bwd in RLOD on L ft, close R ft to L; step fwd in LOD on L ft, hold one Ct, step thru in LOD on R ft turning in to face ptr and assuming Loose CP M's bk twd COH, hold one Ct; grapevine down LOD step swd in LOD on L ft, step on R ft XIB of L (W also XIB), step swd again on L ft, step on R ft XIF of L (W also XIF);

21–24 *Pivot, –, 2, –; Turn Two-step; Turn Two-step; Twirl, –, 2, –;*
In CP M's bk twd COH start L ft and do a couple R face pivot 1 full turn in two slow steps; do 2 RF turning two-steps; M walks fwd two slow steps as W does one slow RF twirl under M's L and W's R hands to end in CP M's back twd COH;

25–28 *(Box) Side, Close, Fwd, –; Side, Close, Back, –; (Breakaway) Side, Back, Fwd, –; Side, Back, Fwd, –;*
Step swd in LOD on L ft, close R ft to L, step fwd twd wall on L ft, hold one ct; step swd in RLOD on R ft, close L ft to R, step bwd twd COH on R ft, hold one Ct; (Breakaway) step swd in LOD on L ft opening out ¼ R to face RLOD in a left open pos, rock bwd in LOD on R ft (L ft remaining in place), rock fwd in RLOD on L ft turning ¼ L to face ptr and wall, hold one Ct; release lead hands and join M's R and W's L hands step swd in RLOD on R ft opening out ¼ L to face LOD in open pos, rock bwd in RLOD on L ft (R ft remaining in place), rock fwd in LOD on R ft turning ¼ R to face ptr and wall in CP, hold one Ct;

29–32 Repeat action Meas 25–28, on last fwd step of Meas 32, M remains facing LOD as W turns ½ L to face M assuming CP, hold one Ct;

Perform entire routine for a total of 2½ times, through Meas 16.

Ending

Twirl, –, 2, –; Apart, –, Point, –;
M walks fwd two slow steps in LOD as W does one slow R face twirl in two steps under lead hands; change hands to M's R and W's L, step diag apart from ptr (M bwd on L and W on R ft), hold one Ct, point M's R and W's L toe twd ptr, hold one Ct.

"BIRTH OF THE BLUES"
(Two-Step)

Composers: Bud and Shirley Parrott
Record: Decca No. 29360
Position: Diag OP-fcg for Introduction, as noted for dance
Footwork: Opp, directions for M except as noted

Introduction

Measures
1–4 *Wait; Wait; Apt, –, Pt, –; Tog CP, –, Tch, –;*
   1–2   In diag Op-fcg wait two Meas;
   3   Step apt on L, –, pt R twd ptr, –;
   4   Step tog on R to CP M fcg LOD, –, tch L to R, –;

Part A

1–4 *Fwd Two-step; Fwd Two-step; (Bjo) Fwd, –, 2 (Check), –; XIB, Side, Fwd, Lock;*
   1–2   CP M fcg LOD do 2 fwd two-steps L, R, L, –; R, L, R, –;
   3   Blend to Bjo M fcg LOD step fwd L, –, fwd R check, –;
   4   XLIB of R (W XIF), step R swd diag twd LOD and wall, fwd L, lock RIB of L (W IF);

5–8 *Fwd, –, Manuv CP, –; Pivot RF, –, 2, –; Trn Two-step; Trn Two-step;*
   5   Bjo stcp fwd LOD on L, –, fwd R trng RF IF of W to CP M fcg RLOD, –;
   6   Do a ¾ RF cpl pivot L, –, R to CP M fcg wall, –;
   7–8   Continue with two RF trng two-steps L, R, L, –; R, L, R to end CP M fcg LOD, –;

9–16 *Repeat Action of Meas 1–8.*

Part B

17–20 *Prog Scis, 2, 3 (Scar), –; Prog Scis, 2, 3 (Bjo), –; Fwd, Lock, Fwd, –; Fwd, Lock, Fwd, –;*

17   CP M fcg LOD step side L, close R, XLIF (W XIB) to Scar, –;
18   Step swd R, close L, XRIF (W XIB) to Bjo, –;
19   Step fwd LOD L, lock RIB of L (W IF), fwd L, –;
20   Step fwd R, lock LIB of R (W IF), step fwd R, –;

21–24 *Repeat Action of Meas 17–20 to End In CP M Fcg LOD;*

Part C

25–28 *Side, Close, Fwd, –; Side, Close, Bk, –; Dip Bk, –; Rec Trn R, –; Piv RF, –, 2, –;*
25   CP M fcg LOD step side L, close R, fwd L, –;
26   Step side to wall on R, close L, step bwd R, –;
27   Dip bwd twd RLOD on L, –, rec fwd on R trng ¼ RF, –;
28   Do a RF cpl pivot L, –, R to end in CP M fcg wall, –;

29–32 *Trn Two-step; Trn Two-step; Twirl, –, 2, –; Pickup, –, 2 (CP), –;*
29–30   Do two RF trng two-steps down LOD L, R, L, –; R, L, R, –;
31   M walk fwd LOD L, –, R (W does 1 RF twirl under joined lead hands), –;
32   M walk fwd L, –, R (W fwd R, –, L trng LF IF of M) to end in CP M fcg LOD, –;

Sequence: Introduction, Parts A, B, C; Parts A, B, C; Parts B, C; Ending.

Ending

1–4 *(SCP) Dip Fwd, –, Rec (CP), –; Dip Bk, –, Rec, –; Trn Two-step; Trn Two-step;*
1   Last time thru Part C end in SCP fcg LOD dip fwd L, –, rec bk on R trng to CP M fcg wall, –;
2   Dip bwd twd COH on L, –, rec fwd on R, –;
3–4   Do two RF trng two-steps down LOD L, R, L, –; R, L, R, –;

5–6 *Twirl, –, 2, –; Apt, –, Pt, –;*
   5   M walk fwd LOD L, –, R (W does one RF twirl under joined lead hands), –;
   6   Change hands to M's R and W's L step apt on L, –, pt R twd ptr to Ack, –;

"MEXICALI ROSE"
(Waltz)

Composers: Jack and Na Stapleton
Record: Grenn 14088
Position: Introduction and dance, open-facing, M facing wall
Footwork: Opp. directions for W unless indicated

Introduction

Measures
1–4 *Wait; Wait; Apart, Point, –; Tog, Tch, –(to Open-facing);*
Wait two meas in open-facing pos, M's R hand W's L hand joined; step apart on L, pt R twd ptr, hold one ct; step diag twd ptr and RLOD on R, tch L to R, hold one Ct ending in open-facing pos M facing wall;

Dance

1–4 *Fwd Waltz; Wrap, 2, 3; Fwd Waltz; Fwd (face), Side, Close;*
Starting M's L and swinging joined hands fwd waltz one meas fwd in LOD; swinging joined hands bwd M does another fwd waltz as he leads W into a full L face turn in three steps to wrapped pos facing LOD joining M's L & W's R hands in front; in wrapped pos waltz one meas fwd in LOD; releasing M's R & W's L hands keeping others joined, step fwd LOD on R (W fwd on L) turning ¼ R (W ¼ L) to face ptr, step side on L, close R to L ending M's bk twd COH M's L and W's R hands joined and extended twd LOD;

5–8 *Twinkle (RLOD); Twinkle Manuv; (R) Turning Waltz; (R) Turning Waltz (to OP-face);*
Swinging joined M's L and W's R hands twd RLOD, twinkle down RLOD stepping L XIF R (W R XIF L), side on R turning to face ptr, close L to R; stepping R XIF L (W L XIF R) twinkle down LOD turning ¼ RF to end in CP M's bk twd LOD; stepping bwd twd LOD on L do two waltzes down LOD making a ¾ RF turn to end in open-facing pos M's bk twd COH;

9–12 *Fwd Waltz; Wrap, 2, 3; Fwd Waltz; Fwd (face), Side, Close;*
Repeat action of Meas 1–4;

13–16 *Twinkle (RLOD); Twinkle Manuv; (R) Turning Waltz; (R) Turning Waltz (to Bfly);*
Repeat action of Meas 5–8 except end in Bfly pos M's bk to COH;

17–20 *Waltz Balance (L); Waltz Balance (R); Vine/Twirl; Thru, Side, Close (to Bfly);*
In Bfly pos step to side LOD on L, step on R behind L (W also XIB), step in place on L; step to side RLOD on R, step on L behind R, step in place on R; as M vines down LOD stepping L, behind L on R, side L, W twirls RF under M's L hand progressing down LOD; step thru twd LOD on R, step to side LOD on L, close R to L to end in Bfly pos M's bk twd COH;

21–24 *Waltz Balance (L); Waltz Balance (R); Vine/Twirl; Thru, Side, Close (to Bfly);*
Repeat action of Meas 17–20;

25–28 *Fwd Waltz; Fwd, Point, –; Solo Turn, 2, 3; Tog, Tch, – (to CP);*
Quickly turning to SCP waltz fwd twd LOD; step fwd on R, pt L fwd and hold one Ct; do a ¾ spot solo turn in three steps with M turning LF (W RF) to end facing ptr; step fwd twd ptr on R (W fwd L), tch L beside R to end in CP M's bk twd COH;

29–32 *Bal Bk, –, –; Waltz Manuv; (R) Turning Waltz; (R) Turning Waltz (to Op-face);*

In CP bal bk twd COH on L and hold 2 Cts; waltz manuv turning ¼ RF to CP M's bk twd LOD; starting bwd M's L do 2 RF turning waltzes to end in open-facing pos M's bk twd COH;

Dance goes through two times.

Ending

On Meas 32 last time thru end in CP M's bk twd COH then add: Bal bk twd COH on L, hold two Cts; twirl W RF, change hands to M's R & W's L, step apart and Ack.

MISS FRENCHY BROWN
(Two-Step)

Composers: Harv and Marge Tetzlaff
Record: Grenn 14182
Position: Open, facing LOD for Introduction, SCP facing LOD for dance
Footwork: Opposite, directions for M except as noted

Introduction

Measures
1–4 *Wait; Wait; Apart, –, Cross Point, –; Together SCP, –, Touch, –;*
   1–2 OP-facing LOD wait two measures;
   3–4 Step apart on L, –, cross point R over L twd COH, –; step tog on R (SCP), –, tch L, –;

Part A

1–4 *Fwd Two-step; Fwd Two-step (Bfly); Side, Close, Fwd, –; Side, Close, Bk, –; (Box)*
   1–2 In SCP do two fwd two-steps;
   3–4 Blend to bfly pos facing wall side L, close R, fwd L, –; Side R, close L, bk R, –;

5–8 *Push Away, 2, 3, Clap; Tog, 2, Turn/ Rise, –; Away, 2, 3, Clap; Tog, 2, 3, Tch (SCP);*
   5   From bfly pos push away from ptr M backing to COH (W twd wall) L, R, L, clap hands;
   6   Both moving fwd M R, L, (R hips adj) turn ½ RF (W LF) rise on ball of R, –;
   7–8 Back away L, R, L, clap; together to SCP R, L, R, tch L;

9–16 *Repeat Measures 1–8 in RLOD—ending in bfly pos M facing wall.*

Part B

1–4 *Side, Close, Side, Close; Side, –, Thru (OP), –; (bfly) Side, Close, Side, Close; Side, –, Thru (OP), –;*
   1–2 In bfly pos facing wall side L, close R, side L, close R; side L, –, thru R to OP facing LOD, –;
   3–4 Blend to bfly pos, repeat Meas 1–2;

5–8 *(Hitch) Fwd, Close, Bk, –; Bk, Close, Fwd, –; Strut Fwd, –, 2, –; 3, –, 4, –;*
   5–6 In OP facing LOD do a full hitch fwd L, close R, bk L, –; Bk R, close L, fwd R, –;
   7–8 Strut fwd LOD L, –, R, –; L, –, R, –;

9–16 Blend to bfly pos facing wall, repeat Meas 1–8 of Part B to end in SCP facing LOD.

Sequence: Parts A, B, A, B, A, Ending.

Ending

1–3 *Fwd Two-Step; Fwd Two-Step; Twirl, –, 2, –; Apart, Point.*
   1–2 In SCP facing LOD do two fwd two-steps;
   3   M walk fwd L, –, R, as W does a RF twirl under joined lead hands to end facing M, –; quick/apart and point as music ends.

TANGO MANNITA

Composers: Manning and Nita Smith
Record: Grenn 14198
Position: As shown
Footwork: Opp, directions for man

Note: A slow step requires two beats of music, a quick step requires one beat of music. Position and facing direction of man are shown at start of each two measures, and changes from this position are indicated in instructions.

Introduction

Meas. Pos. and Facing dir.
1–2 Open, LOD
  1–2 Wait eight beats of music
3–4
  3 Step fwd slow L, step fwd slow R;
  4 M steps fwd quick L as W steps quick R across in front of M as she turns L face to take closed pos, M steps quick R twd wall, draw slow L to R;

Part A

1–2 Closed, LOD
  1 Step fwd slow L, step fwd slow R;
  2 Fwd quick L, side quick R twd wall, draw slow L to R;

3–4 Semiclosed, COH
  3 Step slow L twd COH, step slow R twd COH;
  4 M steps quick L across in front of W as he turns R face to take closed pos facing wall, step quick R twd RLOD, draw slow L to R;

5–6 Closed, Wall
  5 M dip bk twd COH on slow L, recover twd wall slow R;
  6 Fwd quick L, side quick R, draw slow L to R;

7–8 Semiclosed, LOD
  7 Fwd slow L, fwd slow R in LOD;
  8 Fwd quick L as W steps quick R across in front of M as she turns L face to take closed pos, step quick R twd wall, draw slow L to R;

9–16 Repeat Meas 1–8.

Part B

1–2 Closed, LOD
  1 Fwd slow L, cross slow R thru to banjo pos;
  2 Rock fwd quick L, bk quick R, bk quick L, swing R bk as W flares L and turns R face to semiclosed pos;

3–4 Semiclosed, LOD
  3 Rock fwd quick R in LOD, recover quick L in place, fwd quick R, hold;
  4 Fwd quick L as W steps quick R across in front of M as she turns L face to take closed pos, step side quick R twd wall, draw slow L to R;

5–8 Repeat Meas 1–4 of Part B.

Part C

1–2 Closed, LOD
  1 Fwd slow L, fwd slow R;
  2 Fwd quick L, fwd quick R, fwd slow L;

3–4 Closed, LOD
  3 Fwd slow R, fwd quick L, fwd quick R;
  4 Fwd slow L, turn to face wall in closed pos slow R;

5–6 Closed, Wall
  5 Step side quick L in LOD, touch R toe quick in back of L, step side quick R in RLOD, flare L;
  6 Cross quick L in back of R, step side quick R in RLOD, cross quick L in front of R, flare R as both turn to semiclosed pos;

7–8 Semiclosed, LOD
  7 Rock fwd quick R in LOD, recover quick L in place, fwd quick R, hold;
  8 Fwd quick L as W steps quick R across in front of M as she turns L face to take closed pos, step side quick R twd wall, draw slow L to R;

Ending

1 Semiclosed, COH
  1 Fwd quick L, fwd quick R, turn to reverse Semiclosed pos to face twd wall and with joined hands held high do a side corté (dip) twd COH, hold;

Yesterday's Contras for Today

"It was a sensation out of the past—a fleeting glimpse of our dance heritage—like eating homemade ice cream fresh out of an old crank-type freezer," said Stan Burdick, publisher of *American Square Dance* magazine, describing his enjoyment of dancing to the cues of America's "contra master," Ralph Page.

Contras are especially enjoyable because the movements are easy to learn, and the patterns always fit the music phrasing, allowing time for graceful, rhythmic dancing. They are sometimes called longways, or line dances, because they are usually danced from formations of long lines, and sometimes called circle dances when adapted to that formation. Literally, a contra dance is a dance of opposition, a dance performed by many couples, face-to-face, line facing line.

Longways and circle dances were popular with the settlers in all thirteen of the original colonies. They stemmed from three major sources: the English "longways for as many as will," the Irish "Cross Road dance," and the Scottish "reels."

Yet contras have also been updated, with additions of modern square dance movements such as "swing through" and "spin the top." There is a stirring of interest in reclaiming this time-honored dance form and restoring it to a more prominent place in today's dance picture by including one or two on each square dance program. There is also an increase in contra clubs springing up across the land.

A longways "set" for contra dancing is usually made up of four or more male-female couples who form two lines that are about four steps apart. There are various ways of placing the gents and ladies in the lines. In some contras all of the gents are in one line facing the ladies in the other line, each gent across from his partner. In others, ladies and gents are mixed in each line, and partners stand side-by-side facing another couple in the other line.

Still others have dancers all facing toward the prompter. Only the first two formations described will be dealt with here.

A prompter (caller) directs the movements. Prompting a contra is different from calling a square dance because it employs only necessary cue words without fill-in patter. The contra dance has a fixed pattern made up of movements, each of which is usually phrased in eight counts requiring eight full steps for performance. The prompter gives the cue while the preceding movement is being completed.

There is wide variation in music for contras. They are usually danced to jigs, reels, and hornpipes. They are also danced to marches, polkas, waltzes, hoedowns, and square dance singing call tunes. Music for contras should have strong eight-count phrasing.

For arm turns, the pigeon wing or elbow hook, or forearm grasps are appropriate. (See "The Special Language of Square Dancing: A Selected Glossary," and "85 Mainstream Movements with Calls.")

Following are two contras and the directions for dancing them. The counts are numbered in conjunction with the calls. Directions for the square dance movements involved are in the square dance section. Special contra movements are described in detail in the explanations for each of the dances.

The call or "prompt" begins during the introductory musical phrase. Dancing starts later, exactly on the first beat of the first phrase of the melody. Dashes (−) indicate phrases of music during which there is no prompting. After the dancers become familiar with the routine, the prompter need only say the *italicized* words.

Now, line up your dancers, put on a record with strong eight-count phrases—a jig or reel if available, or even a hoedown or popular tune without a vocal—and get ready to "reel the set."

Selected Contras

VIRGINIA REEL

With six couples in the set, men stand side-by-side in a line facing the ladies standing side-by-side in a line, with partners facing, about four steps apart. Positions in the lines are numbered consecutively. Couple 1 stands at the end of the line nearest the prompter, gents to the prompter's right, ladies to the left.

To "reel the set," Couple 1 does a complete right-arm swing around each other; pass by right shoulders, and the lady left turns through with the next gent in line (Gent 2), as the gent does a left turn through with the next lady in line (Lady 2). The lead couple meets in the center to do a right turn through; then they left turn through with the next lady and gent (Couple 3), right turn through with each other, then left turn through the next couple, and so on down the line. After turning the last couple, they follow the next call.

To "sashay," designated couples join both hands (rights to lefts) and sidestep (or sideskip) in the direction indicated.

To "march to the foot," all dancers first face toward the prompter, then ladies follow the head lady, gents follow the head gent, as the first couple separates, the lady going right, the gent left, and each marches down the outside of the line to the foot of the set. Head couple makes an arch with each other, becoming the foot couple. Couple 2 becomes Couple 1 and leads as the others follow under the arch and sashay forward to place in line. Each couple has moved up one position. The dance is repeated until the original lead couple is back in No. 1 place.

Music
Beats,
Steps   *Prompts*

Intro	– – – –,	All *forward*, bow, and back
	Dancing begins	
1–8	– – – –,	Do it *again*
9–16	– – – –,	Turn partners *right hands around*
17–24	– – – –,	Turn partners *left hands around*
25–32	– – – –,	Partners *two-hand swing* (clockwise)
33–40	– – – –,	All *do sa do*
41–48	– – – –,	First couple *sashay down*
49–56	– – – –,	. . . *and* all the way *back*
57–64	– – – –,	. . . and *reel the lines*
1–8	– – – –,	– – – –
9–16	– – – –,	– – – –
17–24	– – – –,	– – – –
25–32	– – – –,	– – – –
33–40	– – – –,	(same couple) *Sashay to head*
41–48	– – – –,	*March* to the foot and *arch*
49–56	– – – –,	Couples *sashay to the head* of the set
57 -64	– – – –,	All *forward*, bow, and back.
	Next sequence begins . . .	

Formation for Virginia Reel.

Formation for Virginia Reel.

SLAUNCH TO DONEGAL

With any even number of couples in the set, partners in standard position (lady at gent's right), couples face couples in long lines down the hall, or in two circles. (In lines, when an end couple, or an end lady in each line, has no one in position with whom to do a particular movement, the couple or lady stands in place for eight counts until the next movement.) Repeat the full sequence six or eight times according to the music duration, or until dancers have returned to original positions.

*Music
Beats,
Steps   Prompts*

Intro – – – –, *Allemande left* (ends are corners)
    Dancing begins
  1–8   – – – –,   *Swing* your partners (twice, then
                   remake lines)
  9–16 – – – –,   *Slant left, right, and left through*
                   (each couple faces the couple
                   diagonally across to their *left,* then
                   right and left through. Two of the
                   end couples wait.)
  17–24 – – – –,   Straight *across, right, and left
                   through*
  25–32 – – – –,   Same four, *two ladies chain*
  33–40 – – – –,   *Chain* them *back*
  41–48 – – – –,   Same four *left-hand star*
  49–56 – – – –,   *Right-hand star* back to lines
  57–64 – – – –,   *Allemande left* your corner.*
    Next sequence begins . . .

* The last time, substitute, "and bow to your partner" for the last line.

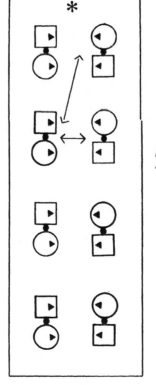

Formation for Slaunch to Donegal.

V

CALLING, TEACHING, CALLS, MUSIC, EQUIPMENT, FEES

Caller in action.

So You Want to Be a Caller

Square dance calling is a folk art.

Anyone with leadership qualities, a clear voice with good pitch, a sense of rhythm, and a strong desire to learn, teach, and call square dances for the enjoyment of others can be a caller.

Calling and teaching are synonymous in square dancing. A caller is not an entertainer, but is the leader who teaches and calls the directions for dancers' movements while they are dancing. This position is unique in folk dancing, as the caller is an essential part of the square dance performance and has the prerogative of changing the order of the movements at will.

Ideally, the would-be caller should be an experienced mainstream club square dancer of at least one or two year's standing and be a graduate of one of the caller colleges conducted by experienced callers. However, most callers start out with far less background in square dancing. A caller does need to understand thoroughly the language of square dancing and the movements required to meet the specific needs of the dances involved. (See "The Special Language of Square Dancing: A Selected Glossary.") These needs vary greatly from group to group.

There are roughly five categories of square dancing and calling skill levels—for programs, parties, classes, clubs, and challenge dancing. One can be a good caller at any level, but any accomplished caller can handle all but the fifth specialized category.

In the first category, dancers learn only one or two complete square dance call routines for presentation on a program (for Scouts, schools, etc.). For them the caller/teacher needs to know the particular movements involved and the appropriate "calls." In the second category, where movements are learned and danced for enjoyment on the same occasion, such as a party or to entertain vacationers at camps, the caller needs to have command of enough of the simpler movements, mixers, and ice breakers to provide an interesting program of the length needed.

In the third category, where those in physical education classes learn and dance for credit in a course, the caller must be thoroughly familiar with enough consecutive movements and calls to fill the teaching time allotted.

The fourth classification, for classes and subsequent square dancing at clubs, festivals, and conventions, requires that the caller have in-depth command of most of the mainstream movements used in modern square dancing.

Calling for the fifth group, skilled challenge dancers, requires further experience and training with ever-changing experimental movements. These are not included in this book because they change frequently.

In addition to knowledge of the fundamentals of square dancing, other attributes contribute to the teacher/caller's success. Most important among these are enthusiasm, a pleasant personality, and patience with learners and dancers. The caller must be able to soothe bruised egos, relax tensions, and cajole a floor full of dancers into co-operation.

A geometric sense of the movement patterns is helpful, as are an open attitude and willingness to study, practice, and learn, along with a sincere desire to introduce people to the satisfaction of joyful self-expression offered by square dancing. Background in other folk dance forms is also beneficial.

The caller is responsible for seeing that the facilities are adequate (either personally or through a sponsoring agency, club, or school). These include a clean, suitable place, with rest room facilities and provisions for quenching thirst. Also needed are appropriate music (square dance records are recommended) and sound equipment (either furnished personally or by the sponsoring agency). The caller must know how to operate the sound equipment efficiently.

It is recommended that the caller set an example by wearing appropriate clothing (square dance attire if training dancers for club dancing) and be present and ready to begin when the dancers arrive. The caller should follow a high code of ethics in relation to other callers and business arrangements with clubs and sponsoring agencies, and use standard nomenclature for calls.

Callers should keep in mind that they are nurturing and sharing with their fellow man a precious part of American heritage—a shining American treasure.

Thus, a square dance caller wears many hats. He or she must at times be a leader, teacher, audio engineer, choreographer, acoustician, psychologist, diplomat, peacemaker, janitor, historian, master of ceremonies—and a supersalesperson.

Many square dance leaders recommend that the beginner caller start out by teaching, and calling for, inexperienced dancers who are not accustomed to smooth, expert calling. The step-by-step instructions in this book may be used for this purpose, as well as serving as a reference and guideline for more experienced callers.

However, the beginner caller must make careful advance preparation. Before the first lesson, he or she should study the movements, pictures, and diagrams until able to envision the action mentally; memorize the "calls"; and practice with music until the words flow as smoothly as in a song. Clear enunciation is a necessity. The actual cue words telling *who* does *what* should be accentuated for clarity. Listening to and studying techniques and timing used at dances by experienced callers and in calls recorded on square dance records are also helpful.

There are two kinds of square dance calls: "patter calls" and "singing calls."

"Patter calls" get the name from the extra words and rhymes added to the actual cue words denoting the movement to be danced.

For "patter calls," the words are spoken with a background of music, in a sort of rhythmic chant. The caller follows the rhythm and tempo of the music while harmonizing in the same key with the band.

Phrasing of the "calls" and dance movements is independent of the phrasing (but not the rhythm) of the music. Although many movements in modern square dancing are designed for performance to four, eight, or sixteen beats of music, these are variable under different circumstances, and there are also many exceptions. Therefore, in setting the timing for the calls to the music, dancers must be given time to perform the action according to the number of steps required at a given time. In order to provide continuous dancing without a break between movements, the call for the movement to follow must come while the dancers are completing the action of the previous call, slightly in advance of the actual performance. This is done by beginning some "calls" in the middle of a musical phrase (but on the beat), or spacing the cue words with fill-in patter, or by waiting the necessary number of beats while dancers complete the movement.

In the diagram that follows, a sample call is shown in relation to the beat of the music and the dancers' steps. Each line is divided into eight parts, representing beats of music; the "call" is in capital letters; and *underlined* numbers show how the dance steps relate to the music and the "call."

There are four parts choreographed into each complete square dance call, whether a patter call or a singing call (see "The Special Language of Square Dancing: A Selected Glossary" for descriptions of the two types of calls). These parts and their usual order are: figure (twice); break; figure repeated (twice); and an ending. In many calls, movements choreographed for the opener are repeated in the break and the ending. Each part begins and ends with partners in home positions.

Choreography is different for patter calls and singing calls. Parts to patter calls are not as sharply delineated, and no set "figures" are choreographed into a particular call. In singing calls, the parts are clearly recognizable, and the same figure is repeated four times.

Although the caller may choose different movements to incorporate into each call, the arrangement of the movements must follow certain established guidelines in order to have a smooth flow of action, interesting choreography, and end up with all dancers back in po-

beats	1	2	3	4	5	6	7	8
call	ALL	EIGHT	FOR —	WARD	AND	COME	ON	BACK
steps					1	2	3	4

dance forward

beats	1	2	3	4	5	6	7	8
call	CIRCLE	TO THE	LEFT	(wait)	A	ROUND	THE	TRACK
steps	1	2	3	4	1	2	3	4

dance back to place   circle to the left

beats	1	2	3	4	5	6	7	8
call	ALL	TURN	BACK	(wait)	GO	SIN	— GLE	FILE
steps	5	6	7	8	1	2	3	4

go half around   all turn back go

beats	1	2	3	4	5	6	7	8
call	BACK	AT	HOME	SWING	(wait)	SWING	WITH	STYLE
steps	5	6	7	8	1	2	3	4

single file   start the swing

beats	1	2	3	4
call	(NEXT "CALL" BEGINS)			
steps	5	6	7	8

finish swing

sition to "allemande left" with their original corners and return to partners in the proper place and sequence.

For a smooth flow of action, if a movement ends by using one hand, the next movement should begin with the other hand, or not involve a handclasp; and abrupt changes of body movement direction should be avoided. For example: "allemande left (hand)" should be followed by a call such as "right (hand) and left grand," or "do sa do" (pass right shoulders), instead of "left hand swing," or "seesaw" (pass left shoulders).

The selection of movements should not be repetitious and monotonous. For example: "Heads pair off, sides dive through, pass through, right and left through" called twice puts dancers back in position and in sequence for "allemande left." It would be more interesting if the first and second times were separated by a movement such as "square through three hands, all California twirl." If the call was interrupted just before the final "right and left through," dancers would be out of place and sequence for the "allemande left."

Callers are generally known as "memory" callers or "sight" callers or a combination of both. All callers should memorize "calls" for individual movements, but "memory" callers are those who memorize arrangements of movements put together by other callers for a complete square dance. "Sight" callers are those who know and can visualize the movements so well that by watching the dancers they can instantly choose and call an appropriate movement. As a rule, beginner callers should start out as "memory" callers.

There is a slight difference in the calls for trained dancers and for learners. Teaching "calls" used for students are more explicit and contain more explanatory words than are needed for experienced dancers. A "teaching call" accompanies the explanation of each of the eighty-five mainstream movements. Each call is combined with appropriate movements that take the dancers from home positions through the movement and back to home positions. Therefore, these calls may be called consecutively in any order of arrangements.

Singing calls are so designated because each one has a set pattern choreographed to exactly fit a particular tune, and they are usually sung instead of chanted. (Sometimes there is more than one pattern for a popular tune.)

The approach to calling singing calls is slightly different from that to patter calls. Singing calls must be selected to fit the dancers' needs—easy ones for beginners and more challenging patterns for experienced dancers. (Occasionally both an easy routine and a complicated routine are written for the same tune, and the same record can be used for both levels of dancing. An example follows later.)

Callers must always make sure that dancers are thoroughly familiar with all of the movements included in the singing call before calling it for them to dance. There is no time to wait for dancers to catch up or to repeat the "call" if they get behind. One good way to make sure they can dance it is to "patter call" the movements first to a hoedown tune for them to practice.

Singing calls are available on square dance recordings accompanied by written copies of the calls. On one side of 45 rpm records, a caller sings or harmonizes the words to the music; on the other side there is music only. A caller may memorize the call as recorded, then play the music side and sing along with it.

Since square dance records and sources are constantly changing, the caller should check for current listings of them in periodicals named in the "Bibliography and Sources of Other Materials." *American Square Dance* and *Square Dancing* magazines carry current listings and regularly provide a dance and record evaluation service. A subscription to *Square Dancing* is linked to membership in the Sets in Order American Square Dance Society. Each year SIOASDS makes available to members three long-playing records, featuring outstanding national callers, which provide good guidelines to the current dancing trends based on mainstream basic movements. The calls are divided into three dancing level categories utilizing (1) the first fifty basic movements, (2) seventy-five basic movements plus ten (eighty-five mainstream movements), and (3) challenge or experimental calls and movements. Other examples of good calling and choreography are demonstrated in the records *"Marshall Flippo Calls the Basic Fifty,"* and *"Marshall Flippo Calls the Seventy-Five Basics Plus"* on the Blue Star label.

In Flippo's "Basic Fifty" record there is a good example of an easy singing call routine set to the tune of "Summer Sounds" for which there is also a more advanced routine (Bob Dawson, MacGregor—2051). The wording as called by Dawson is as follows, with the Flippo changes shown in parentheses.

Summer Sounds

Introduction, Break, Ending

Circle left . . .
Listen to the music of the carousel
The ting-alinga-lingle of the ice cream bell

or,
The paddle of a steamer on a Sunday cruise
The sizzle of a hot dog at a barbecue

or,
Shrieking of a roller coaster away up high
The whistles on the beach as a peach walks by

Allemande left your corner, your partners do sa do
Gents star left once around you go
(All promenade)

Do sa do the partner, with the corners allemande
Come back and promenade the land

Here come summer sounds, the summer sounds I love.

Figure

Heads (Sides) . . .
Star through, pass through, circle round the
    track
(Four Ladies promenade, go once inside the
    ring)

Head men break and make a line, go forward
    up and back
(Gents swing your partner, yes, swing that
    pretty Jane)

Pass through, wheel and deal, centers star
    through
(Allemande left your corner, do sa do your
    own)

Pass through, clover leaf, the new center two
(Four Gents promenade one time around you
    roam)

Square through, three quarters, turn corner by
    the left
(You do sa do the partner, and your own lady
    swing)

All the way around, promenade this pet
(Swing your girl and promenade that ring)

Here come summer sounds, the summer
    sounds I love.

What expenses and remunerations are involved in becoming a square dance caller?
Both vary widely according to the situation,
the skill and reputation of the caller, and the
ability of the square dance group to pay.

A schoolteacher or camp leader could be
furnished the necessary instruction books, records, and sound equipment, and not receive
extra pay for teaching or calling for students
or campers. A hobbyist might buy his or her
own equipment and call gratis occasionally on
a club program or as a service to civic groups.

But a person getting into calling for clubs on
a regular basis will spend hundreds of dollars
and many hours of time on equipment and
training. It will probably take several years of
diligent, consistent effort to earn back from
caller's fees the initial investment.

As a dancer, the would-be caller discovered
that few recreations offered so much for so little cost. The dancer needed only buy a western
shirt or a full-skirted dress, pay an admission

fee, and settle with the baby sitter. The outlay
from the other side of the microphone is quite
different.

Standing up front in full view instead of
being hidden in the crowd requires better and
costlier costumes. There are textbooks, notes,
and magazine subscriptions to buy, dues for
local caller organizations, and tuition to a
caller's school or institute to be paid for.

The learning process never stops for the person who wants to be a caller for modern
square dancing. Nationally known callers often
spend more time in research and study than at
the microphone before the dancers.

A public-address system is a necessity (variable turntable recommended). They cost anywhere from $150 for an older used set up to
$1,000 for one of the complete, finely crafted
electronic miracles on the market today. A
used microphone to start out with can sometimes be found for $15 to $25; new ones are
higher.

Square dance records cost over $2.00 each,
and a dozen would be a minimum number
needed to start—six hoedowns for patter calls
and six with singing calls. All records must be
selected to fit the voice range and preferences
of the caller. This is usually done by trial and
error. The caller should determine which key
fits his or her voice best, then select music ac-
cordingly.

Caller and paraphernalia.

Payment ranges from a token fee of $5.00 or less to a local caller for an evening of calling for a small group, up to $150 to $300, or a percentage of the ticket sales, plus travel expenses for a top-rate traveling caller who conducts an afternoon or weekend workshop and calls for an evening dance that attracts hundreds of dancers from a wide area. Clubs usually pay club callers according to the size of the membership and their outside expenses, such as the cost of the hall. This ranges somewhere between $15 and $50 for calling a regular club dance.

When setting up to call or teach, ideally the caller-teacher stands near the music source—record player or musician(s)—at the end or side of the dance area, preferably facing the entrance from a platform or stage in order to be able to watch the dancers' movements. A microphone is helpful even with small groups, but it is necessary for larger gatherings, as the voice must be clearly understood above the sound of the music.

Here are some teaching tips.

Make out a lesson plan in advance, but remain flexible. During some sessions dancers learn faster; at others, the pace is slower.

Don't forget that this is recreation from the first call of "Square your sets" to the final "That's it, that's all." It is the responsibility of the caller (teacher) to make it enjoyable by using a pleasant tone of voice and cajoling instead of commanding the dancers to do the movements.

After dancers are in place, explain the position designations, and have each dancer raise a hand when his or her's is called out. Suggest that each dancer note who partners and corners are so that when they meet across the square they will recognize each other by those designations.

Emphasize that the modern square dance step is a smooth, gliding walk without skips or jerks.

Be sure that dancers understand that only designated dancers are to be active and that inactive dancers stand in place and do not change the direction faced unless directed, or unless the movement calls for an automatic counterpart action.

Then, without music, slowly and with pauses for dancers to orient themselves to changes in position, direct the dancers, one move at a time, in a "walk-through" of the movement until each is thoroughly familiar with it. Now you are ready to start the music and call the movement while the dancers enjoy performing it in time to the music. Be sure to enunciate clearly and distinctly.

After several movements have been learned, they can be combined in a continuous call. The caller should mix the order of presentation to encourage the dancers to listen closely and to keep them from anticipating the calls. Watch the dancers at all times and be aware of their positions and performance. Call each new movement while dancers are just completing the previous one so they will not have to stop and wait to find out what to do next.

When one of several squares has "broken down" (dancers are out of place and cannot perform the movements), make it clear that those dancers must immediately return to home positions, wait for a movement in the "call" that begins from that position, then take up the dancing from there, instead of expecting the caller and other dancers to stop just for them. If several sets break down, the caller should stop the music, request dancers to return to home positions, and all start over.

Allow dancers to rest about every twenty minutes. And don't forget to tell them often, "You're looking great, you're doing fine."

Marshall Flippo (right) top U.S. traveling caller, gives pointers on styling to Japanese dancers at the 23rd National Square Dance Convention.

VI

LET'S GET ORGANIZED

Clubs, Classes, Costs, and Camaraderie

Square dancing is purely for pleasure. Those who have already learned to "curlique" and "square through" with ease, and those wishing to master the fine points of "swing through," want only to find some friendly square dancers and join the fun.

These friendly dancers are found in square dance clubs. Clubs are the adhesive that holds modern square dancing together.

Yet for newcomers or visitors to a community, locating a club and learning which night it meets and where, sometimes takes a bit of sleuthing. That is because square dancing is not commercial or competitive; therefore news media publicity is often scant and scattered. In some communities square dancers do have a listing in the telephone directory.

If not, a few questions here or there will usually produce the information needed. Likely sources are: chambers of commerce, YMCAs, churches, recreation departments, gas station attendants, waitresses, and police.

Square dance clubs have two main functions. Once dancers learn how to square dance, clubs provide a place and an opportunity to enjoy the newfound recreation on a regular basis—usually weekly or twice monthly; and they are most often the sponsoring agents for the classes necessary to perpetuate and expand the activity. Membership in a club opens the door to the wide, wide world of square dancing. Members are eligible to attend most other clubs across the nation and overseas. There are clubs for fraternal groups, youth and children, solo (unmarried) dancers, senior citizens, campers, handicapped dancers (deaf, those in wheelchairs, blind), and foreign nationals and Americans in other countries.

Sometimes clubs are begun by members of classes sponsored by a recreation department or other organization such as a Sunday school class or a fraternal group. Others start when a few friends get together, find a caller/teacher, select a club name, and meet regularly for the

"Right and left grand . . ."

purpose of square dancing. Clubs organize into area, state, and national associations.

Club names are often colorful and descriptive. Some examples are: Grand Squares, Belles and Beaus, Dudes and Dolls, Kalico Kickers, Kerchief and Calico, Rip-snorters, Sashayers, Teen Twirlers, Saints and Sinners, Solo Squares, and Yellowrockers.

The way dancers become qualified for club membership is determined by club members. One way is by completion of the prescribed number of lessons sponsored by the club. Another is by having been a member of another club.

Administrative needs of most square dance clubs are few and functional. The organization and by-laws should be tailored for the group involved, keeping in mind that the chief objective is the enjoyment of square dancing. Clubs may be administered either by the dancers, the caller, or an executive committee. Usually a president, vice president, treasurer, and secretary can handle the club business with the help of a few appointed committees.

Leaders need to secure a caller, who will probably provide the necessary equipment (sound system, records, and record player); arrange for an adequate meeting place (recreation hall, patio, or converted storeroom); establish weekly or bimonthly meeting dates; and set and collect club membership dues. Most clubs are nonprofit organizations exempt from paying taxes. Therefore dues are kept low, as they need only meet the expenses involved—caller fee, building rental, simple refreshment costs, and a small miscellaneous fund for items such as stamps, stationery, and publicity. Necessary records need to be kept—treasury reports, minutes, disbursements, caller and building rental contracts (if any), and correspondence.

A club name should be selected and a badge designed and ordered for each member. The badge should show the name and location of the club and the dancer's first and last names on it. The same design often is used on a club banner. This banner is displayed at club meetings. Many clubs have an extra traveling banner, which is sometimes "stolen" by friendly dancers visiting from another club. The only way to retrieve the banner is for a full square to attend one of the visitor's club dances and "steal" it back.

The leaders establish standards of dress and etiquette and instigate a system of membership rotation for social responsibilities (hospitality and refreshments at regular meetings and for special or holiday affairs).

Those in charge also work out details for sponsoring classes. As a rule these are held annually or biannually. Leaders secure a teacher (often the club caller), arrange for a place, set dates, provide publicity (posters, radio, newspaper, etc.), and set fees. Fees, prorated to meet costs, are kept low. Officers also outline a plan utilizing members, who are called square dance "angels," to serve as "helpers" with the classes.

Courses designed to prepare dancers for modern club-level square dancing are usually set up in 2- or 2½-hour sessions held one night a week for from twenty to thirty meetings. On completion of the course the club

Although unable to see, this gent was a full-fledged member of several square dance clubs (note badges).

usually holds a graduation dance complete with some kind of nonsensical initiation into the club membership, such as requiring them to dance with shoe boxes on their feet. Other clubs are invited to join the festivities and extend a friendly welcome to the new dancers.

The costs of square dancing classes and club membership are in a moderate range. Classes usually cost $1.00 to $1.50 per person a lesson —less than many movies. After classes comes membership in a club that meets on a regular basis two or four times per month. Dues are seldom more than $5.00 monthly per couple.

Special dances are held periodically, and the cost varies from $1.00 to $3.00 per person. This pays for approximately three hours of enjoyable entertainment, often to the calling of a nationally known caller.

Square dancers have a special friendly feeling for other square dancers. The Texas State Federation of Square and Round Dancers furnishes a little brochure for new dancers that describes this camaraderie as follows:

"It is rather difficult to describe the average square dancer. They come from all walks of life and are good, clean, tolerant, and lovable citizens.

"Square dancers enjoy a camaraderie and common ties found in very few groups of people. To another square dancer, wherever he may be, your only recommendation to him need be that you are a square dancer.

"If you happen to be in a strange town, find a square dancer and you have found a ready-made friend. He'll only want to know your first name, where you are from, and 'would you like to dance tonight?' If there is not a regular dance, a few couples will get together and show you a whopping big time. Sorta makes you feel funny way down deep.

"Some square dancers even keep spare bedrooms for the visiting dancers, and their home is the visitor's home—all with no recommendation other than that the visitor is a square dancer.

"Square dancing is not merely executing calls to the beat of the music. It is more than that. It is something one feels within one's self. You acquire a sense of "belonging" that gives deep satisfaction.

"So you see that it is hard to describe square dancers. Even if you never square dance, your life would be richer for having known them. We'll just leave it this way: You'll never regret entering into the fun and fellowship that will be yours as a square dancer."

Costumes, Courtesy, and Styling

One can enjoy square dancing and round dancing while wearing cut-off jeans and sweat shirts, evening gowns and tuxedos, or Japanese kimonos. But for classes or informal practice sessions, most ladies wear low-heeled shoes and comfortable, casual clothes. A lightweight dress (or blouse) with a loose skirt is recommended. Gents don't need a coat or tie, as slacks and a sports shirt (long-sleeved as a courtesy to prevent ladies grasping a perspiring arm) will do.

For club and festival dances, special colorful traditional square dance costumes are more festive and appropriate. Functional, comfortable, and attractive square dance clothing of similar but widely individualized styling has evolved over the years and has come to be accepted as the proper square dance costume. These costumes have been called "happy clothes" because they show that the wearer is all set for an evening of enjoyable recreation, and they establish an atmosphere of relaxation and conviviality.

For ladies, this costume consists of pretty, personalized, color-co-ordinated garments— dress, petticoat, pettipants, and shoes. Dresses are usually made of lightweight and washable fabrics, with or without designs. The general style has a fitted bodice with any desired type

Fluffing petticoats for a camping square dance.

of sleeves and collar, and a wide skirt—full circle or more, either gathered, gored, or tiered. Decorative trimming may be braid, lace, ribbons, or ruffles. The length varies according to popular street-length styles, but a standard length just covers the knees.

Underneath there is a bouffant half slip with several gathered tiered layers of Dacron, nylon net, or marquisette that flares and ripples during the dancing to occasionally reveal fitted, thigh-length, usually elasticized, pettipants

Colorful, co-ordinated square dance costumes.

trimmed with rows and rows of dainty lace. Some petticoats have up to one hundred yards of material in them.

Low-heeled square dance slippers, with a band over the instep for comfort, complete the costume. Wearing of bracelets, wristwatches with dangling chains, and large rings with sharp edges is discouraged, as they might cause injury or be accidentally broken.

Gents wear slacks or western dress pants that lend themselves to being accessorized with hand-tooled belts and fancy buckles. Well-fitted western-style shirts with small pearl grippers are enhanced by a bolo, gambler, string, or beaded tie. Shirts always have long sleeves and are either regular factory-made models of any color, or are tailor made to match the partner's dresses. Some men wear solid-color shirts with a vest that matches the partner's dress.

Footwear for men ranges from regular dress shoes or handsome hand-tooled cowboy boots to a shortened ankle-high boot developed especially for square dancers.

Costumes are available from square dance specialty shops, some of which are advertised in the magazines listed under "Bibliography and Sources of Other Materials." Many dresses are tailor made—either by the wearer or a local seamstress. Pattern books have square dance dress patterns, and other suitable styles that may be adapted.

Dancers in specific groups, such as clubs and exhibition teams, often design distinctive matching costumes that they all wear on special occasions. At the national square dance conventions there is usually a state costume available for those who wish to obtain and wear it.

Courtesy practiced at square dances establishes a friendly, comfortable atmosphere for enjoyable recreation. Square dancing is a casual activity, and there are no strangers at a club or class meeting. No formal introductions are needed—dancers just step right up and call each other by first names and dance together in a square the first time they meet. Learning names is easy because everyone wears a name tag.

Personal hygiene is very important to square dancers because of the vigorous physical exertion required and the close proximity of dancers in a square. Most dancers find it necessary to apply effective underarm antiperspirant deodorants, and are careful not to eat highly spiced foods, such as onions or garlic, before a dance in order to avoid embarrassment caused by odors offensive to others.

Square dancing requires total application of the faculties and co-operative teamwork. Therefore, drinking alcoholic beverages just prior to or during a square dance is not practiced.

Although square dancing is an energetic activity, it is not to be performed in a rough manner causing discomfort to other dancers. Courtesy and consideration are the criteria observed.

All square dancers soon learn not to talk during instructions and calls. They must also learn to listen. Without hearing the call, the movements can't be danced. A dancer who does not understand an instruction should feel free to ask for additional explanation from the instructor, but not from a dancer while in the square.

When a dancer "goofs" by missing a call, causing the set to "break down," all dancers cheerfully return to home positions and wait for a movement that begins from that position to continue dancing. Each one knows that he or she might be the "goofer" the next time.

It is considered good manners for dancers to fill any vacant place in a square near them instead of passing it by for another. Prearranging the makeup of a set, or leaving one set to join another, is considered rude.

Caller/teachers do their best to see that everyone has fun at class and club dances. Dancers can reciprocate by telling them, "That was a great dance, thanks for calling for us."

Styling is the specific way dancing is performed—the smoothness, gracefulness, hand and body positions. In addition to styling taught by the caller/teacher, the dancer should observe the following styling suggestions:

1. Perform movements and step smoothly and courteously in time to the music.

2. Keep the body erect and dance with the weight over the balls of the feet.

3. Men hold free hands and arms close to the body. If ladies' hands are free, when wearing full skirts they flare their skirts out at the sides by holding them.

4. Dancers should learn the standard hand position for each movement and perform it properly, for comfort and to avoid confusion. They should use only a light pressure when joining hands or forearms. Joined hands are held just above the lady's waist level, and elbows are kept near the body at a 90-degree angle when executing forearm turns or swings.

5. When dancing with a new group, a courteous dancer observes and adopts any differences in styling.

Demonstration and Exhibition Dancing

Although square dancing is a participation performance, as opposed to a spectator sport, dancers occasionally like to show off their favorite recreational activity on programs for seated audiences or for other dancers. It can be done effectively in several ways.

Sometimes a spontaneous informal demonstration presents dancing just as it is done at a modern club dance, with dancers wearing regular square dance costumes. Another time, for a special occasion, a smooth-flowing exhibition of carefully selected and practiced movements choreographed with elaborate flourishes is staged to present pleasing precise geometric figures, with dancers wearing specially designed (often identical) costumes. Or perhaps authentic old-time figures danced in pioneer costumes are appropriate for the occasion, such as a historical pageant or program.

Whichever type of presentation is chosen, dancers and their caller should be aware that they are representing all square dancers. They should employ enjoyable showmanship, graceful square dance styling, good taste, and effective staging when displaying the rhythmic pleasure and teamwork of this popular recreation.

Appropriate entrances and exits are a part of any square dance presentation on a program. They and the movements to be danced should be worked out and rehearsed in advance so that dancers may be able to find their positions easily and perform smoothly.

The movements should be carefully chosen, keeping in mind how it looks to the observer, rather than featuring the skill of the dancers in performing complicated maneuvers that may look like chaotic confusion to the nondancer. The clean geometric lines of a simple "star promenade" or "bend the line," done with exacting precision, is more pleasing to the spectator's eye than the most intricate mixtures of "square throughs" and "swing throughs." A good exhibition has an eye-appealing balance among formations of stars, lines, squares, and circles.

When "Pappy" Shaw served as dance consultant for the movie *Duel in the Sun*, Darryl F. Zanuck, the director, objected to using the "right and left grand" in the dance scene. He thought the movements were not pleasing to the eye. "Too much push me, pull me," he said.

Dancers should present a unified performance by agreeing in advance on the number and timing of swings and twirls and other flourishes. All should use the same hand positions for promenades and arm turns, etc. Skirtwork (ladies holding skirts out at one or both sides), lifts, and symmetrical formations add to the beauty of a spirited, flowing performance if performed simultaneously and gracefully. An interesting variation might include dancing the two-step, polka-step, or tap dance clog step during part or all of the presentation.

If costumes are not matched, they should be somewhat uniform in general style and appearance. Trousers and shirts similar in color, and dresses which are the same length from the floor present a more unified appearance.

When ladies' hands are free and they hold the skirt out, they should be careful to center their grasp at the sides so the back or front won't hike up. Gents should practice holding their hands near their hip pockets, with elbows close to the body when not using them in the movements. When making stars or circles, arms should be held curved and above waist height. Lines and stars and circles should be as geometrically perfect as possible.

The caller is an essential part of square dance exhibitions. Every effort should be made to have a "live" caller rather than a recording with a set call on it. Most recorded calls are designed for club dancing and have repetitions of "allemande left" and "right and left grand," which should be kept at a minimum in an exhibition. The presence and voice of a caller add an extra dimension to the performance. A participating caller can exercise more leeway in choosing movements that are interesting to watch, and in case of mistakes, can change the call a bit and rescue the performance.

The caller's costume should be appropriate for the type of exhibition, and his call should be clearly and distinctly projected with enthusiasm, so it can be heard by the audience as well as the dancers. The call needs to be as carefully prepared as the choreography of the dance. A sloppy call with poor timing, long silences, or aside remarks thrown in detracts from the program. Exhibitions sometimes show special movements such as "grand square" or "teacup chain"—for which there are no specific calls. The caller should fill in

with lively patter while they are being danced.

The fifteen "Oldies but Goodies" are selected adaptations of movements. They may be danced separately to demonstrate dancing as it was done in earlier days; or combined, to present a medley of movements. Costumes may be copies of pioneer dress, typical of modern square dance wear, or matched dresses and shirts for all four couples.

Following is an example of a well-balanced medley of movements suitable for a modern exhibition dance. It can be danced as it is, or changed to suit the needs and inclination of the performers. In rehearsal, precision should be emphasized as much as possible—keeping lines straight, using uniform hand positions, etc.

The caller starts the music and announces with enthusiasm, "Here come the square dancers, let's

Promenade one, promenade all
Square your set(s) in the middle of the hall."

The patter should continue until dancers have reached previously determined positions. (If Couple 1 stands with backs to the audience and is the first to start a couple movement, all other dancers will be more or less facing the audience.)

The movements only are listed here. Complete "calls" for individual movements accompany their introduction in fifteen "Oldies but Goodies."

All swing. Circle left.
All turn back promenade single file.

Make a (left-hand) spinning wheel. Turn back.
Make a (right-hand) spinning wheel.

Gents turn back and partners swing.
Promenade to places.

Sides face, grand square.
(Fill in with patter unless directional calls are needed).

Heads face to (the couple at) the right
(sides automatically face couple at their left).
(This pairs Couple 4 with Couple 1, and Couple 2 with Couple 3 in facing diagonal lines.)

Right and left through. Right and left back.

Heads face to the left (sides face right).
(This pairs Couple 1 with Couple 2, and Couple 3 with Couple 4 in facing diagonal lines.)

Right and left through. Right and left back.

Gents left-hand star. Pick up partners for star promenade.
Make two stars (ladies drop off in a right hand star).
(Lady 1 should start into the star from No. 4 position, as she will be facing the audience to begin with.)

Go twice around (in separate stars).
Change stars (ladies cross in front of partners).
Go twice around.

Gents pick up partners, star promenade.

Heads wheel around two. Sides wheel around two.
Heads wheel around two. Sides wheel around two.
Courtesy turn to place.

Teacup chain (the caller fills in with patter).

Heads flap the girls. Heads circle. Swing.
Sides flap the girls. Sides circle. All swing at home.
(Inactive dancers step back a few steps, squat down on the floor, and lead the applause when the girls are lifted, then quickly return to place for the swing.)

"All circle to the left and do it well
Into the center with a cowboy yell (yipee)
Circle to the left around the floor
Into the center and yell once more

Now bow to partners and corners all
And wave to the folks (audience) and that'll be all.

Promenade right off the floor
That's all there is, there's not any more."
(Couple 1 leads off in a previously set direction.)

Associations, Festivals, Conventions, Publications, Archives, and Foundation

Square and round dance organizations offer dancers an opportunity to enjoy their recreational hobby across the nation and overseas. There are club, association, roundup, festival, and convention dances. Archive centers and The Lloyd Shaw Foundation record and perpetuate the activity.

More than 150 area publications provide an excellent service to dancers and callers by listing club, class, and special dances within their specific readership areas. *Square Dancing* and *American Squares,* magazines with national distribution, also frequently note special events. In 1974, in order to provide a handy guide to these dances and establish a service for newcomers or travelers seeking an opportunity to dance in an area, Bob Osgood, editor of *Square Dancing* magazine, organized a worldwide listing of square dance "information volunteers." In each August issue, *Square Dancing* publishes a directory of these volunteers and a listing of pertinent information.

The 1974–75 *Directory of Square Dancing* gives this information about the listing:

"Represented in the listings are all of the United States, the Canadian Provinces and some 33 Countries abroad where square dancing is being enjoyed. For reference and convenience, under each State, Province or Country listing are the current contacts, as we have them, for (1) Square Dancer Associations and Councils of Associations, (2) Callers Associations, (3) Round Dance Leaders Associations, (4) Archives Centers and (5) Area Publications. Finally (6), are the Information (Info) Volunteers. These are the men and women who are ready to provide dance information on square dance events in their areas.

"What are the Archives Centers? A growing number of areas and groups have established centers where complete files of *Square Dancing* and other square dance publications are available for reference and study. The goal is to eventually have these centers in use in all major square dance communities. Those with old square dance books, records, manuscripts, etc., which they would like to make available to others, are invited to contact an archives center near them or the Central Archives Center in care of this publication, 462 North Robertson Boulevard, Los Angeles, California 90048."

The Lloyd Shaw Foundation is a chartered, nonprofit foundation with the started objective: "To recall, restore and teach the folk rhythms of the American people: in dance, music, song, and allied folk arts, as a tribute to the memory of [the late] Dr. Lloyd Shaw."

Lloyd Shaw became an internationally known educator because of an unusual program that combined a very sound academic curriculum with a remarkable program of extracurricular activity that was designed for lifelong usefulness and immediate joy. Dr. Shaw was deeply concerned about the need for an almost constant program of wholesome activity for the whole student body—not just the athletic teams—in order to drain off safely the volatile physical and emotional energies of the children.

Summer classes in American folk dancing were held at Cheyenne Mountain School near Colorado Springs, where he was superintendent for thirty-five years. The foundation now has three workshops a summer at three widely separated universities: Colorado State University, and two others in varying locations from year to year. The workshops offer classes, mostly for young teachers, in how to present the American folk dance at two levels: elementary children, and teen-agers and adults.

Dorothy Shaw (Dr. Shaw's widow) and Fred Bergin, owners of Lloyd Shaw Recordings, which produces records and instructional material, donated material to start the foundation. Their address is The Lloyd Shaw Foundation, Inc., P. O. Box 203, Colorado Springs, Colorado 80901.

Since 1952 an annual National Square Dance Convention has been arranged and staged entirely by volunteers. The national executive committee tells what a national convention is all about:

"The National Square Dance Convention is the world's greatest square dance event. What makes this so? That the square dancers find a superb place to enjoy dancing to the very best callers, is but frosting on the cake. Sure there are reunions of friends, a chance for a family vacation, and, of course, lots of fun. However, the real name of the game is education. Each year the role of education within the National is gaining in importance and purpose. This is rightfully so. The National is the mecca for furthering ideas of leadership, calling, functions, and organizational aspects of the basic unit of square dance—the club. Here is developed the philosophy and role of square, round, and contra dancing for this wonderful hobby."

National conventions are held the last weekend in June each year. Previous and projected locations are as follows: Riverside, California, 1952; Kansas City, Missouri, 1953; Dallas, Texas, 1954; Oklahoma City, Oklahoma, 1955; San Diego, California, 1956; St. Louis, Missouri, 1957; Denver, Colorado, 1959; Des Moines, Iowa, 1960; Detroit, Michigan, 1961; Miami Beach, Florida, 1962; St. Paul, Minnesota, 1963; Long Beach, California, 1964; Dallas, Texas, 1965; Indianapolis, Indiana, 1966; Philadelphia, Pennsylvania, 1967; Omaha, Nebraska, 1968; Seattle, Washington, 1969; Louisville, Kentucky, 1970; New Orleans, Louisiana, 1971; Des Moines, Iowa, 1972; Salt Lake City, Utah, 1973; San Antonio, Texas, 1974; Kansas City, Missouri, 1975; Anaheim, California, 1976; Atlantic City, New Jersey, 1977; Oklahoma City, Oklahoma, 1978; Minneapolis, Minnesota, 1979.

A report by the publicity cochairmen of the twenty-third National Square Dance Convention held June 27–29, 1974, in San Antonio includes the following information.

Total registration as of 9 P.M. Saturday evening was 18,100. Dancers from all 50 states and 9 foreign countries attended, including 76 from Japan (6 callers and a round dance leader), representatives from Canada, Germany, Saudi Arabia, Canal Zone, Puerto Rico, Switzerland, Mexico, and the Philippines.

Square dancing in six halls offered several levels of dancing. Dancers ranged in age from 4 to 85. Over 8,000 "do sa doed" in the street by the Alamo.

Twenty-four exhibition groups performed, including square dancing, round dancing, clog steppers, tap dancing, and contra dancing. There were 22 "after" parties.

The "Story of Square Dancing" was told in a variety show. Afterward there was a square dance wedding in the theater with dancers as guests and the family squaring up on the stage following the ceremony. The Style Show drew a capacity audience.

The Showcase of Ideas boasted sixty organizations exhibiting from the United States and Canada, a Hall of Fame Art Collection, and over 339 publications on display. The International Room was decorated with 76 banners of clubs from outside the United States. Mountains of petticoats and other square dance wares were on sale in 134 booths.

The KLRN educational TV station filmed thousands of feet of film for a documentary. The convention was given coverage by the local news media and *Woman's Day* magazine.

The Sew-and-Save panel featured over 3,000 participants—models and instructors. Solos (single dancers) registered over 800. Campers numbered about 1,500 in 515 camping units. The Youth Room was jammed with over 1,000 square and round dance enthusiasts. Eighty round dance leaders from all states and Japan helped with cuing and monitoring; and there were 450 volunteer square dance callers. There were 29 panels, clinics, and seminars.

The Parade of States and Countries filled the huge arena floor as thousands cheered the colorful sight that kicked off the grand finale dance. The security police report stated, "We've been looking for trouble but just can't find any. The happiest convention we've ever had."

Altogether, the associations, festivals, conventions, publications, archives, and foundation help pull the square dance movement together. They promote, protect, and perpetuate this significant facet of American heritage.

VII

SQUARE DANCING FOR
YOUTH AND CHILDREN

"Dive through . . ."

Tie in with Tomorrow

"The answer to the question 'Where do we go from here?' seems to lie in the direction of a new generation of square dancers—teenagers and pre-teens—who have been discovering in their hobby a sensible, enjoyable and challenging approach to growing up. They are the ones who will carry the fun into the future.

"More than just a recreation, square dancing serves to develop many of the social responsibilities of young America. Courtesy, tact and leadership are just a sampling of the qualities derived from participation in this very non-'square' activity." (*Youth in Square Dancing, Sets in Order Handbook Series.*)

Square dancing offers the shy youngster a comfortable place in group activity and gives the extrovert a chance to let off steam—all in an atmosphere of fun and enjoyment. A child psychologist once said to a group of parents and teachers, "Square dancing is an ideal recreational activity for youth and for children. Vigorous enough to offer fine physical exercise, it also promotes rhythm and grace in growing bodies, develops desirable social behavior and provides social acceptability, and furnishes just the right amount of touch contact to satisfy normal boy/girl relationships. I recommend it as a basic part of every child's school experience."

Youth and school-aged children are capable of learning and enjoying most of the same square dance movements that adults dance. Usually it is agreed, however, that adults, youth, and children should not dance together in mixed squares on a regular basis, as it tends to detract from the pleasure of all three groups. Young dancers may be divided into natural maturity groups rather than according to school grades. Children are generally more comfortable with children, teen-agers find more pleasure dancing with their peers, and adults enjoy dancing with adults.

A factor to consider in relation to modern-day square dancing is that mastering the many complicated movements required for adult club dancing requires between twenty-five and thirty two-hour sessions of instruction and practice. Students seldom have that much time and interest to apply to one particular activity in their busy schedules. Therefore in their own groups they can enjoy dancing those traditional and modern movements that they have time to learn, and at the same time establish the basis for a pattern of wholesome recreational activity that can be continued into adulthood.

There are also other special considerations. Young boys and girls are shy about doing movements calling for putting their arms around each other. They usually have not developed the muscle control needed for comfortable co-ordination of movements required in close body contact, such as the waist swing and star promenade, which are danced with arms around each other's waists. These problems can be eliminated by substituting a two-hand swing for the waist swing, and an "elbow hook" for around-the-waist arm positions. On the other hand, older youth who have no objection to these positions are more energetic than mature dancers and enjoy doing more vigorous movements—such as "lifts," extra "twirls," hand-clapping, and other flourishes.

Children six to eleven or so dance more joyously if allowed some freedom to skip and hop and if they are not required to be too precise. For them the simple beginning movements, and traditional figures found in 15 Oldies but Goodies, are more appropriate.

From age eleven or twelve, young square dancers find satisfaction in more complicated movements. High school students and older youth usually have good co-ordination and can, with practice, perform intricate movements with skill and pleasure. Many youth clubs across the nation are dancing at top adult level. They dance in their own squares at local and state association dances, and "have a

"Allemande thar . . ."

"Swing your pretty girl . . ."

ball" dancing in the special youth program held as part of the National Square Dance Convention each year.

Junior high and high school square dance programs are usually more successful if supported by student leaders such as the student body president, or a popular athlete. Adult leaders should make every effort to maintain a close balance between boys and girls in the group.

Courtesy and consideration should be practiced by the teacher and encouraged among the students. Instead of bluntly pointing out mistakes, embarrassment can be avoided by a kindly explanation to the erring student that it was "almost" right. After all, if they wrongly extend the left hand instead of the right, they did extend a hand, didn't they? And each student should be equally tolerant of "goofs" by

other dancers, because next time they might be the "goofers."

Parental support should be enlisted if possible, especially in the instance of establishing a club. Their understanding of the aims and needs involved in the program—practice hours, costumes needed, necessity for regular attendance—is essential to a good program. After a leader has carefully nurtured an attitude of appreciation for the activity, it is disappointing if parents don't encourage regular attendance.

In general, with adult supervision and leadership, the same criteria apply to youth and children's groups as to adults. The same tips to callers, costuming, etiquette, club organization and square dance fun, with step-by-step teaching procedures detailed elsewhere in this book are appropriate for use with children.

Bibliography and Sources of Other Material

This book is essentially concerned with *modern* square dancing and round dancing except for the material in "Background of the Modern Square Dance." Most of the information was gleaned from the sources listed below, current regional periodicals, and personal observation of the activity's development since the late 1940s to its present state, although many current regional periodicals and outdated books and pamphlets were researched. Current officers for the organizations listed are given.

American Square Dance (magazine), Box 788, Sandusky, Ohio 44870.

Burleson, Bill. *Square Dancing Encyclopedia,* 2565 Fox Avenue, Minerva, Ohio 44657.

Callerlab, International Association of Square Dance Callers; Bob Osgood, Executive Secretary, 462 North Robertson Boulevard, Los Angeles, Calif. 90048.

Canadian Dancers News (magazine) 578 Pleasant Park Road, Ottawa, Ontario, K1H5NI, Canada.

CROWD (Central Registry of World Dancers), Marv and Syl Leibowitz, 213 Winn Avenue, Universal City, Tex. 78148.

Davis, Bill. *The Top Ten (Movements) 1974–75,* 180 North Castanya, Menlo Park, Calif. 94025.

Evans. *Round Dance with Alf and Elizabeth Evans,* 7208 Nelson Avenue, Burnaby, B.C. V5J 4C3, Canada.

Hamilton, Frank. *Roundance Manual.* SIOASDS (see below).

IRDC (International Round Dance Council), 5 Chicagoland R/D Leaders Society, Sonja Sekulich, 3940 North Nordica Avenue, Chicago, Ill. 60634.

Legacy (Square Dance Co-ordination), Stan Burdick, Box 788, Sandusky, O. 44870; Charlie Baldwin, Box N.C., Norwell, Mass. 02061; Bob Osgood, 462 North Robertson Boulevard, Los Angeles, Calif. 90048.

New England Square Dance Caller (magazine), Box N.C., Norwell, Mass. 02061.

Northern Junket (magazine), 117 Washington Street, Keene, N.H. 03431.

Overseas Dancers Association, Fran and Steve Stephens, 151 Dryden Drive, San Antonio, Tex. 78213.

Sachs. *World History of the Dance,* 1937, W. W. Norton & Co., Inc.

Shaw, Dorothy, *The Story of Square Dancing,* Sets in Order Handbook Series, 462 North Robertson Boulevard, Los Angeles, Calif. 90048.

Shaw, Lloyd. *Cowbody Dances,* Caldwell, Id.: The Caxton Printers, Ltd. 1939.

———*The Round Dance Book,* Caldwell, Id.: The Caxton Printers, Ltd. 1948.

Square Dancing (magazine), 462 North Robertson Boulevard, Los Angeles, Calif. 90048.

The Basic Movements of Square Dancing— Basic 50, SIOASDS (see below).

The Extended Basic Movements of Square Dancing (51–75), SIOASDS (see below).

The Lloyd Shaw Foundation, Mrs. Dorothy Stott Shaw, Box 203, Colorado Springs, Colo. 80901.

The National Square Dance Convention Executive Committee, Loren Long, President, 6901 S.E. 14 Street, Lot 35, Des Moines, Ia. 50320.

The Round Dancer (magazine), 1250 West Garnette, Tucson, Ariz. 87505.

SIOASDS (The Sets in Order American Square Dance Society), Bob Osgood, 462 North Robertson Boulevard, Los Angeles, Calif. 90048.

Index

Printed in the United States
24741LVS00002B/137-142